Better Homes and Gardens®

Paint It!

101 ideas, designs, & patterns for decorating any surface

Better Homes and Gardens® Books
Des Moines, Iowa

TABLE of contents

Better Homes and Gardens® Books
An Imprint of Meredith® Books

PAINT IT!

Editor: Carol Field Dahlstrom
Technical Editor: Susan M. Banker
Graphic Designer: Angela Haupert Hoogensen
Copy Chief: Terri Fredrickson
Managers, Book Production: Pam Kvitne,
    Marjorie J. Schenkelberg
Contributing Copy Editor: Arianna McKinney
Contributing Proofreaders: Karen Brewer Grossman,
    Colleen Johnson, Sherri Schultz
Photographers: Andy Lyons Cameraworks,
    Peter Krumhardt
Technical Illustrator: Chris Neubauer Graphics, Inc.
Electronic Production Coordinator: Paula Forest
Editorial and Design Assistants: Judy Bailey,
    Kaye Chabot, Mary Lee Gavin, Karen Schirm

Meredith® Books
Editor in Chief: James D. Blume
Design Director: Matt Strelecki
Managing Editor: Gregory H. Kayko

Director, Sales, Special Markets: Rita McMullen
Director, Sales, Premiums: Michael A. Peterson
Director, Sales, Retail: Tom Wierzbicki
Director, Book Marketing: Brad Elmitt
Director, Operations: George A. Susral
Director, Production: Douglas M. Johnston

Better Homes and Gardens® Magazine
Editor in Chief: Karol DeWulf Nickell

Meredith Publishing Group
President, Publishing Group: Stephen M. Lacy

Meredith Corporation
Chairman and Chief Executive Officer: William T. Kerr

Chairman of the Executive Committee: E. T. Meredith III

GET THOSE paints AND brushes READY!

Whether you paint projects to decorate your home, to give as gifts, to sell, or just for fun, painting is a creative outlet that has possibilities galore. Our goal is to inspire you with clever projects, tempt you with brand-new techniques, and guide you along with step-by-step instructions and tips from the painting pros.

You can start small with a simple painted place mat or tile, or jump in with both feet to create a magical gourd Humpty-Dumpty or a woodburned and painted park bench. The projects that pull at your heartstrings are the ones you should pursue.

The valuable information in each chapter about paints, brushes, and color—along with specific tips unique to each project—will ensure that you'll have the time of your life painting all kinds of projects.

So whether you mastered painting long ago or are new to this colorful world of self-expression, we guarantee each project in this book to be fun and doable. Come along and open your creative mind to new products and approaches, unique surfaces, and extraordinary ways for using paint. As a clever person who likes to make things and paint them, you're in for a spectacular treat!

Happy Painting!

Carol Field Dahlstrom

All of us at Better Homes and Gardens® Books are dedicated to providing you with information and ideas to create beautiful and useful projects. We welcome your comments and suggestions. Write to us at: Better Homes and Gardens Books, Crafts Editorial Department, 1716 Locust Street—LN112, Des Moines, IA 50309-3023.

If you would like to purchase any of our crafts, cooking, gardening, home improvement, or home decorating and design books, check wherever quality books are sold. Or visit us online: bhgbooks.com

Cover Photograph: Andy Lyons Cameraworks

Permission to photocopy patterns and create projects for individual use and sale is granted by Better Homes and Gardens® Books.

painting TIPS

START SIMPLE

Here's a list of basic painting supplies you're likely to find useful. Most are available at arts and crafts supply stores.

- PAINTBRUSHES
- BRUSH TUB to store brushes and to hold water (A brush tub does double-duty by allowing you to store brushes at your painting station in addition to rinsing them. You easily can get by with rinsing your brushes in cups or jars.)
- SHARP PENCIL OR STYLUS (double-ended is best) to transfer patterns
- SANDPAPER (100- and 150-grit) to prepare surfaces
- TACK CLOTH for removing dust from surfaces
- PAPER TOWELS for blotting brushes (Cotton rags work as well as paper towels. The rags also can be moistened for wiping off sanding dust if you don't own a tack cloth.)
- PLASTIC FOAM PLATE OR TRAY to use as a throwaway palette (Freezer paper is a great alternative to a palette.)
- WOOD SEALER/FINISHER to prepare wood surfaces for paint
- CHALK for transferring patterns
- TRACING PAPER for transferring patterns
- MASKING TAPE for holding patterns in place and masking off areas where paint is not desired (Read the label as some should not be left on a project for more than a day; others will not leave residue on a project when left on for up to a week.)

CHOOSING PAINTBRUSHES

The first time you browse for brushes, you may be overwhelmed by the extensive variety of shapes and sizes. Before you dive into the brush display, keep in mind that you need only a handful to begin. Your best bet is to opt for high-quality brushes, despite their expense. They'll last longer and yield superior results. If you're just starting out, consider a sponge brush for sealing, base-coating, and finishing; a few flat brushes for base-coating and highlighting; and at least one round brush and one liner brush for applying details and lettering. When selecting brushes for a project, a basic rule is to use the sizes that best fit the design areas.

Natural vs. Synthetic

Natural kolinsky red sable hairs are unsurpassed for absorbency and strength. They are the standard by which the industry judges all brushes (including synthetic ones).

With today's technology that enables a variety of fibers to be produced at a reasonable cost, synthetic brushes, which are best suited for acrylic paints, have become the popular choice.

Manufacturers usually assign sizes to brushes by the metric measurement of their flattened ferrule openings. (The metal ferrule connects the brush head and the handle.) For example, a #1 brush measures 1 millimeter, and a #8 brush is 8 millimeters. Anything less than 1 millimeter is designated by the number of units less than a millimeter. A #10/0 liner, for example, measures 10 units less than 1 millimeter.

If you've ever wondered why one manufacturer labels a brush ¼ inch and the next manufacturer calls it a #6, it's simply because one chose the metric system, while the other selected familiar fractions.

Most decorative painters have a variety of brush shapes in their painting supplies. Not everyone knows the name of each shape or what it was designed to do. Refer to these descriptions to identify brushes.

- FLATS: They're ideal for blending, floating, and blocking in large areas of color. You'll recognize flat brushes by their squared-off bristles.
- ANGULAR FLATS: Because the bristles are trimmed at an angle, you'll find these special flat brushes excellent for getting into tight corners.
- ROUNDS: These full-bristled brushes work great for filling in small areas and for applying stroke work. With a little bit of practice, you can vary the pressure on the brush bristles to create both thick and thin strokes.
- LINERS: For a fine, sharp point or for continuous lines of even thickness, you'll find that liner brushes fill the bill.
- SPOTTERS: These are condensed versions of the liner brush with fewer and shorter bristles. Try them for tiny details.
- SCRIPT LINERS: The opposite of a spotter, these liners have extremely long bristles. They hold a lot of thinned paint for line work and script writing but require practice for accurate use.

Some crafters consider these brushes a luxury, but once you've tried them, you won't be without them.

- FILBERT: The softly rounded bristles of this brush resemble the petals of a daisy. With little effort and only one stroke, you can form perfect flower petals or feathers.

- **DEERFOOT STIPPLER:** Here's a full-bristled brush cut at an angle and designed for pouncing on fur, trees, and foliage.
- **ONE STROKE:** With a little practice, you'll depend on this long-bristled flat brush for applying lettering.
- **FAN:** Appropriately named because of its shape, the fan brush works great for dry-brushing grass and foliage or for blending edges.
- **RAKE:** The bristles of a rake brush (also called a comb) "finger." In other words, they split when loaded with paint. You'll find it the perfect tool for creating realistic fur, hair, beards, mustaches, and more.
- **MOP:** Similar in appearance to a wide cosmetic blush brush, this tool aids in blending, it softens shading, and it can be used for antiquing.
- **SCRUFFY:** Just when you think a brush has outlived its usefulness, it becomes an invaluable tool for stippling foliage, beards, and fur.

CHOOSING PAINT

When selecting paint, start with primary or medium-value colors. Throw in a few bottles of basic black and white, and the possibilities for mixing colors are endless. Expand your collection further with an array of premixed colors.

The paint you choose largely depends upon the surface on which you are painting. There are paints made specifically for metal, wood, glass, and other surfaces. Some paints need a primer coat and/or a top coat as a sealer. Consult the paint manufacturer's instructions when selecting paint. Remember not to limit yourself to supplies found in crafts supply stores—be sure to check out what's available in automotive shops, home centers, hardware stores, and discount stores.

CHOOSING COLORS

Whether you are decorating a room or creating a handmade work of art, choosing colors is integral to the outcome. The color wheel can help you understand why some colors work together while others seem to clash. Colors that sit adjacent to one another on the wheel will blend quietly. To enliven a color, add one from the opposite side. All colors alter in appearance when placed next to different colors. Any color will gain importance as you add more of it to an arrangement.

- **PRIMARY COLORS:** yellow, red, blue
- **SECONDARY COLORS:** orange, violet, green (halfway between primary colors on color wheel)
- **TERTIARY COLORS:** yellow-orange, red-orange, red-violet, blue-violet, blue-green, yellow-green (between primary and secondary colors on color wheel)
- **NEUTRAL TONES:** white, gray, black, beige
- **TINT:** made by adding white to a color (For example, pink is a tint of red.)
- **SHADE:** made by adding black to a color (For example, maroon is a shade of red.)

For some ideas on how colors affect mood, see page 111.

TRANSFERRING PATTERNS

Here are three methods for transferring patterns after tracing the outlines of a design on tracing paper. You may prefer one of the following methods over another, depending on the surface of the item you will be painting.

- **Method 1**

Rub the back of the pattern with a No. 2 pencil. Hold the pencil horizontally on the paper while applying the graphite. Lightly wipe off the excess graphite dust. Then place the pattern, pencil side down, on the surface and retrace the lines.

- **Method 2**

Apply the pattern with transfer paper. Check crafts or art supply stores for artist's transfer paper. Avoid carbon paper as over time it will bleed through paint. Slide the sheet of transfer paper, treated side down, between the pattern and the surface; trace over the lines.

- **Method 3**

Make your own transfer paper. You'll need tracing paper and several pieces of chalk, both white and colored. To make light sheets of transfer paper to use on medium- and dark-colored surfaces, rub one side of each piece of tracing paper completely with a piece of white chalk. Use colored chalk to make transfer paper for light-colored surfaces. If you use artist's pastel chalk, its wax base can mar your painting. Rub the chalk into the paper with your fingers. Then shake off any excess chalk. Slip this sheet between the surface to be painted and the pattern. Trace over the design.

PAINTING SMART

It is always a good idea to test paints on a desired surface before beginning. Humidity, newness of paint, project surface, and other circumstances can interfere with the application process.

Be sure to keep paints out of the reach of children. While most of today's paints are nontoxic and are appropriate for use by children, always remember safety comes first.

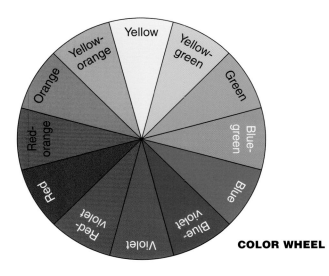

COLOR WHEEL

PAINTING ON glass AND ceramic surfaces

SMOOTH AND NONPOROUS, GLASS AND
CERAMIC SURFACES LET THE PAINT GLIDE ON WITH EASE.
DEPENDING ON THE PAINTS, COLORS,
DESIGN, AND TECHNIQUE USED, YOU CAN ACHIEVE
A SUBTLE OR A VIBRANT EFFECT. GET YOUR
PAINTS AND BRUSHES READY BECAUSE YOU
ARE ABOUT TO BE INSPIRED! THIS CHAPTER IS FILLED WITH
FUN PROJECTS, SUCH AS TABLES, DINNERWARE,
VASES—EVEN A SINK THAT'S AS LOVELY
AS A SPRING BOUQUET.

TIPS FOR PAINTING ON glass AND ceramic surfaces

SELECTING PAINTS

Painting on glass and ceramic surfaces is more fun than ever because of the variety of products available. Look at the selection in arts and crafts supply stores. Once you have decided on a project, keep in mind how the object will be used and cleaned. These are important factors when choosing the type of paint to use.

Another important factor is whether the painted surface will be in contact with food. If you are painting items such as dishes, be sure to choose an appropriate paint. Our dishes on the following pages are painted on the back side so, when in use, the paint does not touch any food.

Read the paint label thoroughly before making a purchase. The type of surface you are painting on may require a special type of paint and possibly a primer or top coat.

SURFACE PREPARATION

Use the paint manufacturer's instructions as guidelines for preparing the surface before painting. The instructions may suggest washing the item in soapy water or wiping the surface to be painted with rubbing alcohol or vinegar. Follow the instructions and then avoid touching the areas to be painted. Oils from the skin may prevent the paint from adhering to the surface.

If a clear primer or surface conditioner is recommended for the paint being used, apply that first where needed. Let it dry.

USING JAR PAINTS

Be sure to shake or stir the paint before using. Many paints separate and need to be mixed for proper application. If the paint is thick, you may wish to thin it slightly with water.

When using the pure, unmixed paint, you may want to remove the lid and use the paint right from the container to eliminate waste. However, do not leave the lid off for an extended period or the paint will dry out. Also be sure the paintbrush is clean or you could alter the color of the paint. Wash or change brushes for each color. When finished, replace the lid securely to extend the life of the paint.

Most glass and ceramic paints are water based and can be mixed together to achieve other desired colors. When mixing paints, place small amounts on a disposable foam or paper plate and

then mix as desired. Mix small amounts or the paint will dry out and be unusable.

As with any paint, the colors will mix when applied next to each other. If you wish to avoid this, be sure to let one paint color dry before adding another. Also let paint dry when applying layers. Most glass and ceramic paints dry to the touch rather quickly, so try to avoid rebrushing painted areas.

Use a paint marker for drawing lines or adding written words to your project. These are usually available in the same area of the store as the paints.

If you make a painting mistake at the start of a project, you can rinse it off the glass or ceramic piece. If necessary, repeat the cleaning preparation steps described on the paint label.

Once the painting is completed, let the piece dry thoroughly. If a clear top coat is recommended, apply it and let it dry.

BAKING/CURING

Some glass and ceramic paints need to be cured in the oven. That means you must bake your painted project in the oven for the paint to become permanent. The paint manufacturer may state that the paint is suitable for the dishwasher after baking. While this may hold true, it is a good idea to gently wash by hand whenever possible.

If baking a painted piece in the oven to cure the paint, be certain it has dried thoroughly beforehand. Usually the paint manufacturer will recommend placing the piece in a cool oven and then turning on the oven. If baking more than one piece at a time, be sure the items are not touching. If the paints on two pieces touch, they may adhere during the baking process. When the painted item has baked for the proper amount of time, turn off the oven and let the painted piece cool inside the oven.

CLEANUP

Most glass paint can be cleaned up with water. To clean paintbrushes, run water over the bristles until the water runs clear. Then reshape the bristles and let dry on a paper towel or bristle end up in a jar. Be sure to clean the sink with an appropriate cleaner when done.

Although many of today's paints are nontoxic and appropriate for use by children, be sure to keep all paints out of the reach of children.

garden-fresh dishes

SET YOUR TABLE WITH ONE-OF-A-KIND

DINNERWARE THAT'S AS FRESH AS SPRINGTIME BLOOMS.

USE HOME AND GARDENING MAGAZINES

AND BOOKS FOR INSPIRATION WITH THIS

TECHNIQUE THAT'S AS EASY AS PAINT-BY-NUMBER.

Glassware can be purchased as a new set or can be mix-and-match pieces from a flea market, garage sale, or secondhand shop. When selecting items for this project, be sure the glass is clear and unscratched. Because the painting is done on the back side, be sure the surfaces to be painted are smooth, including the backs of plates and saucers, and the outside of bowls and cups.

The flower patterns for this project were photographs in home and gardening books and magazines. Other design sources include greeting cards, wrapping paper, and fabric. As long as the picture can lie flat, it can be used.

Additional themes that would work well for this project are pictures or photos of fruit, vegetables, and geometric patterns. Designs with too much detail should be avoided because of the painting technique used.

instructions continued on page 12

Clear glass dinnerware
Newspapers
Home and gardening magazines or books
Small round, flat, and fan paintbrushes
Disposable plate
Glass paints in black and other
  desired colors
Paper clip

garden-fresh dishes

A

HERE'S HOW

1 Wash and dry the dishes according to the paint manufacturer's instructions. Avoid touching the areas to be painted.

2 Cover the work surface with newspapers. For patterns, select large, single flowers from gardening publications, or use photographs you've taken. Place a dinner plate *upside down* on the photograph of the flower. You will be painting on the back side of the plate.

3 Place small amounts of desired paint on a disposable plate. Using the flower as a guide for color and shape, paint in the shape using the corresponding colors as shown in Photo A. The colors that are applied first will be in front when the plate is turned over to the right side. When the painting is completed, use the tip of a paper clip to scratch in details, removing paint in these areas as shown in Photo B. Let the paint dry.

B

THIS REVERSE STYLE OF PAINTING IS A FUN PROCESS
THAT CREATES A MAGICAL SURPRISE ON THE FRONT
OF EACH GLASS PLATE AND SAUCER.

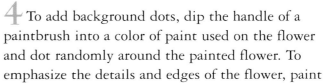

4 To add background dots, dip the handle of a paintbrush into a color of paint used on the flower and dot randomly around the painted flower. To emphasize the details and edges of the flower, paint over the scratched areas with a dark color as shown in Photos C and D. Let it dry.

5 Paint over the flowers and dots using black. Use a fan paintbrush to soften the painted edge as shown in Photo E. Let the paint dry.

6 For bowls and cups, add dots to sides and bottoms as for the plates. Paint the bottoms a color if desired. Let the paint dry.

7 Bake the glassware in the oven if instructed by the paint manufacturer. Let cool. Follow the paint manufacturer's instructions for washing the dishes.

pretty posy sink

WHAT YOU'LL NEED

Ceramic sink in desired color
Tracing paper; pencil; scissors; tape
Paintbrushes
Surface conditioner, such as Delta
  CeramDecor Perm Enamel
Ceramic paints, such as Delta CeramDecor
  Perm Enamel, in desired colors
Clear gloss glaze, such as Delta CeramDecor

TIPS BEFORE YOU BEGIN

Choose a ceramic sink in a desired color and shape. You can adjust the patterns on *page 18* to fit just about any size sink. An almond-colored sink provides a neutral background for all the paint colors shown. If you prefer to use white or another color, you may want to adjust the paint colors so they do not blend in with the sink color.

If the sink has a tendency to roll while you are working on it, place old towels around the sides to steady it. You can also cut a hole in a heavy cardboard box and set the sink in it while painting, creating a temporary countertop. If the faucet is in the sink, tape a plastic bag over it and place tape over the plug area to avoid paint drips.

You can use the patterns on *page 18* as shown, *opposite*, use just some of them, or paint the sink freehand using the patterns as inspiration. If you want to rework an area, use a damp cloth to remove unwanted wet paint.

instructions continued on page 16

AS GLORIOUS AS A FIELD OF WILDFLOWERS, THIS HAND-PAINTED

SINK SHINES WITH COLORS AND DESIGNS FROM MOTHER

NATURE'S COLLECTION. USE ALL OF THE PATTERNS ON

PAGE 18 OR THE DESIRED COMBINATION TO CREATE A

FLOWER-FILLED SINK FOR YOUR FAVORITE POWDER ROOM.

TURN THE PAGE FOR THE INSTRUCTIONS.

pretty posy sink

HERE'S HOW

1 Wash and dry the sink according to the paint manufacturer's instructions. Avoid touching the areas to be painted.

2 Depending on the size and shape of the sink, you may wish to modify the arrangement of the designs shown on *page 14*. You may also adapt the paint colors to coordinate with your home. Trace the desired patterns, *page 18*, onto tracing paper. Cut each motif apart. Use a soft pencil to color over the traced lines on the back side of the tracing paper. Tape each pattern piece in place. Retrace over the pattern lines as shown in Photo A. Remove the patterns from the sink.

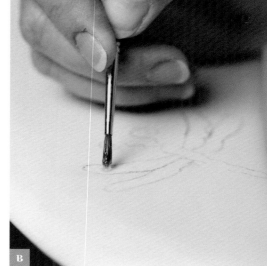

3 Use a clean, dry paintbrush to apply a generous amount of surface conditioner onto the outlined areas as shown in Photo B. Let dry. The sink designs must be painted within four hours or the surface conditioner will need to be reapplied.

USE DEEP SHADOWS TO MAKE THE MOTIFS POP OUT
ON A BEIGE BACKGROUND. IF USING A WHITE SINK, ADD A
TOUCH OF COLOR TO THE WHITES TO MAKE THEM STAND OUT.

16

4 Begin by painting the dragonflies, referring to the color guide on *page 19*. Paint the wings and body white as shown in Photo C. While wet, blend in blue and purple shadows as shown in Photo D. Add leaves and flowers in the same manner. Add a flowing vine using two or three colors of green. Add some small round purple and pink flowers by dipping a round paintbrush into both colors and dotting onto the sink. Let dry.

5 Add thin, dark shadows throughout the design using black as shown in Photo E. Let the paint dry.

6 Top-coat the painted areas with glaze. Let dry. Add a second coat if necessary. Let dry. Let the sink air-dry for 10 days before using.

Note: Clean the sink with a nonabrasive cleanser. Do not leave the sink full of water for long periods of time.

SINK PATTERNS

SINK PAINTING COLOR GUIDES

color burst table

THIS PURCHASED ROUND GLASS TABLE BECOMES

A WORK OF ART WHEN DABBED WITH VIBRANT

GLASS PAINTS. THE BLACK LINES GO ON FIRST,

MAKING IT EASY TO COMPLETE.

Tracing paper

Pencil

Round glass tabletop (available in various sizes in home furnishing and discount stores)

¼ inch flat paintbrush

Glass paints in black, yellow, yellow-orange, orange, pink, purple, bright blue, blue-green, green, blue, red, and magenta

Disposable foam plate

Small round paintbrush

Wrought-iron or other table base

Additional round glass tabletop and clear plastic disks (about the size of a nickel, they are available in hardware stores), optional

HERE'S HOW

1 Enlarge the pattern on *pages 22–23* to the size of the glass tabletop. Trace the pattern onto tracing paper.

2 Wash and dry the glass tabletop. Avoid touching the areas to be painted. Place the glass on top of the pattern, aligning the round edge.

3 Using a flat paintbrush, paint each pattern line on the glass black as shown in Photo A. Paint the edge black. Let the paint dry.

4 Using the paint diagram as a guide, paint a two- or three-color combination inside each of the outlines using the paints listed in the color key on *page 23*. To apply colors to glass, place a small amount of each color on a disposable plate without mixing the colors. Dab the round paintbrush into each color. Dab the colors onto the glass, letting them blend naturally as shown in Photo B. Keep the colors within the black outlines. Let the paint dry. If instructed by the paint manufacturer, bake the painted tabletop in an oven. Let cool.

5 With the painted side up, place the tabletop on the base. If desired, place a second round piece of glass on top of the painted one to protect paint. Place clear plastic disks between the sheets of glass to avoid shifting.

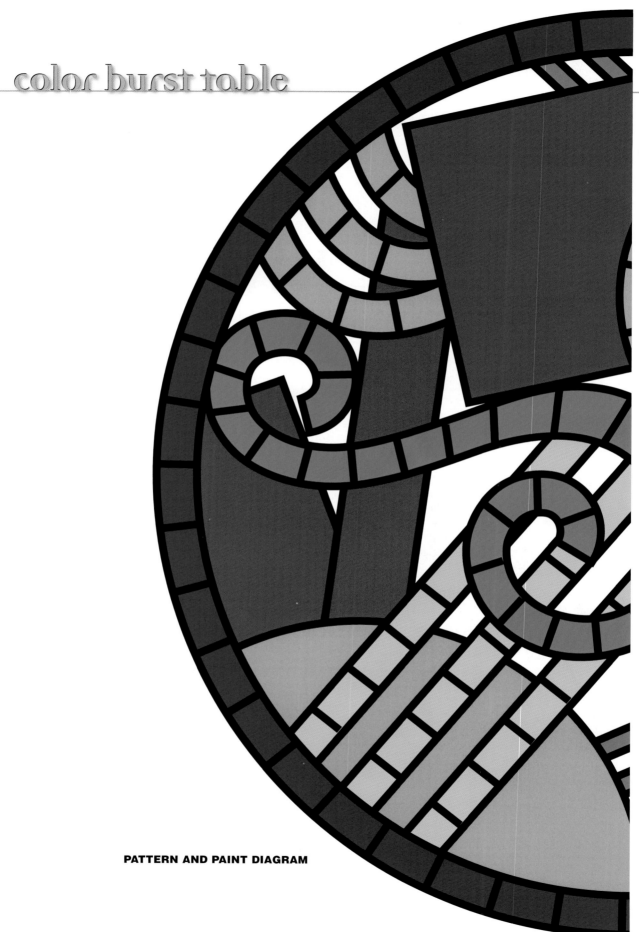

PATTERN AND PAINT DIAGRAM

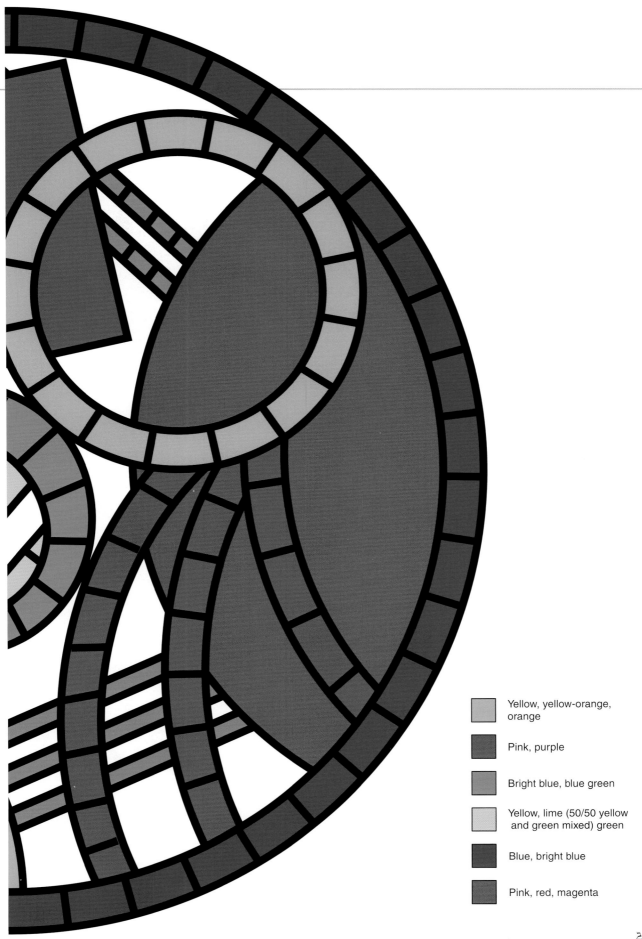

Yellow, yellow-orange, orange

Pink, purple

Bright blue, blue green

Yellow, lime (50/50 yellow and green mixed) green

Blue, bright blue

Pink, red, magenta

tropical tile

Floor tiles are sold in a variety of sizes and colors at home improvement and flooring stores. If making several tiles to give as gifts or to be used for a kitchen backsplash, it may be more economical to purchase tiles by the box.

For this project, a tile with a fairly light, neutral tone works well; however, you can purchase tiles that have dark backgrounds as well. If working on a dark background, you may wish to forgo painting the background color.

The tile pictured is fairly smooth. While a tile with a lot of surface texture may give a more vintage look, it will be more difficult to paint. If you prefer the vintage look, try lightly sanding the dry, painted tile with fine sandpaper. This will allow the tile background to show through the paint in any raised areas.

If you would like to hang a painted tile on the wall, you can adhere a hanger to the back, use a plate hanger, or have the tile professionally framed.

If these colors do not blend with your decor, adjust them as desired.

instructions continued on page 26

Tracing paper; pencil; tape
8×8-inch tan tile
Medium round paintbrush
Glass or ceramic paints in white, yellow
ocher, red, magenta, purple, olive green,
and dark green
Disposable foam plate
Water; toothbrush; paper towel
Fine liner paintbrush
Stand or easel for tile

DISPLAY YOUR TALENTS ON A KITCHEN

TRIVET FOR ALL TO ENJOY. WHILE THIS TILE WAS

CREATED USING GLASS AND CERAMIC PAINTS, THE

STILL LIFE HAS A WATERCOLOR APPEARANCE. TURN

THE PAGE FOR THE INSTRUCTIONS AND PATTERN.

tropical tile

HERE'S HOW

1 Trace the full-size pattern, *opposite,* onto tracing paper. Color the back of the paper with a soft black pencil. Tape the paper onto the front of the tile. Transfer the pattern onto the tile by tracing the drawing with a sharp pencil. If the tile surface is too rough to take the transfer, you can also cut out the images and trace around them onto the tile. Paint the design using thinned white paint as shown in Photo A.

2 Place small pea-size dabs of paint onto plate. Thin the paint with water to the consistency of thin syrup. It should go onto the surface looking like transparent watercolor, only slightly thicker.

3 With water only, paint in a background area, laying water onto the tile with a full brush so that it sits on top of the tile. In areas, let the tile show through the paint. Dip brush in paint and dot onto the water background as shown in Photo B. The adjacent paint colors will spread and blend into each other. Use the paint sparingly at first. Add more color as desired to increase intensity. Let dry. The painting should be done loosely and quickly, not using a lot of brushstrokes.

4 Lightly splatter different colors onto the background area by dipping the bristles of a toothbrush into paint; then rub a finger across the bristles to splatter the paint.

5 To paint the shadows below the fruit, use a thin layer of purple with a tiny touch of green.

6 To paint the grapes, paint a base color of magenta. When it begins to soak in but is still wet, add purple shading as shown in Photo C. Paint one grape at a time. Be consistent in shading with purple on the top left of each grape. Allow the paint to dry before painting next to it, or paint will run together.

7 To paint the green pineapple leaves, paint a base of dark green first. Shade in dark areas with

TILE PATTERN

purple as shown in Photo D. To lighten or highlight, clean the brush, dry it off on the paper towel, and brush off the green paint in areas you want lighter. When you do this, brush once, rinse brush, wipe off on paper towel, and repeat. Add spots of yellow ocher in these areas if desired.

8 To paint the pineapple, paint a smooth, even coat of yellow ocher over the whole oval of the pineapple area. The paintbrush should be full with paint, almost dripping. Paint ocher generously enough that the paint sits on top and does not immediately soak in. Add shading when the paint begins to soak in but is still wet. Clean the brush, dry off on paper towel, and dip

in dark green. Lightly brush the green onto the left side of the pineapple to shade and create shape. Do the same with purple, creating more definition. Paint in the crossed lines using dark purple while ocher paint is still wet.

9 Paint the apple in the same manner, painting a base coat of red and shading with purple and a little dark green.

10 Paint in finer lines, darker shading, and details using a fine liner brush with dark green and purple paints. Add small transparent white highlights onto the pineapple, grapes, and apple in upper right portion as shown in the photograph on *page 24*.

frosted for flowers

PERFECT FOR HOLDING SWEET SENTIMENTAL
BOUQUETS, THIS BEAUTIFUL VASE CAN BE FINISHED
EASILY IN ONE CAREFREE EVENING.

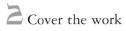

HERE'S HOW

1 Wash and dry the vase as instructed by the glass paint manufacturer. Avoid touching the areas to be painted.

2 Cover the work surface with newspapers. Using a 1½-inch paintbrush, paint a thick coat of etching cream over the outside surface of the vase as shown in Photo A. Etch the vase according to the etching cream directions. Rinse the etching cream off the vase until the water runs clear. Let the vase dry.

Large clear glass vase with wide opening
Newspapers
Etching cream
1½- and 1-inch-wide flat paintbrushes
Disposable plate
Glass paints in white, purple, periwinkle, and sky blue
Pencil with round eraser

3 Place a small amount of each color of paint on a disposable plate. Begin with one color and paint small squares randomly on the inside of the vase as shown in Photo B. Change to a second color, adding more squares and overlapping slightly. Repeat with the remaining two colors. Paint squares on the outside surface of the vase as shown in Photo C.

4 To add dots, using all paint colors except white, dip the eraser of a pencil into the paint and dot onto the outside surface of the vase as shown in Photo D. Let dry.

5 Bake the vase in the oven if instructed by the paint manufacturer. Let cool. If the paint used is not washable, do not fill the vase with water. Instead, place a clear plastic liner in the vase before filling it with water or use the vase for silk flowers only.

little-lady bug tiles

YOU WON'T MIND HAVING THESE SILLY BUGS INCHING
THEIR WAY ALONG THE COUNTERTOP! TRY BRIGHT
GOOD-MORNING COLORS OR USE WHATEVER
GOES WITH YOUR KITCHEN'S COLOR SCHEME.

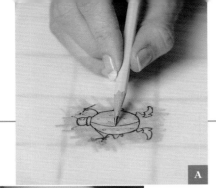

*Small, matte-finish tiles
   (available in home center stores)*
Tracing paper; tape
Pencils with soft and hard leads
*Glass or ceramic paints in green, blue, orange,
   yellow, red, and pink*
Small round paintbrush
Fine black permanent marker
Medium-point black paint pen
Soft, damp cloth
Spray- or brush-on glaze sealer
Tile glue; grout in desired color

HERE'S HOW

1 Wash and dry the tiles according to the paint manufacturer's directions. Avoid touching the areas to be painted.

2 Trace the full-size patterns, *page 33*, onto tracing paper. Using a soft lead pencil, color the back of the traced designs. Tape each pattern onto a tile. Trace around drawing with a very sharp, hard pencil to transfer drawing onto tile as shown in Photo A.

3 Remove the pattern. Paint in sections with a small round brush, using the painting color guides, *page 33*. Let the paint dry.

4 To paint solid-color tiles, thin the glass paint just enough to make it transparent. Paint the desired number of tiles a solid color. Let dry.

5 Use a black marker to outline each drawing and add small details as shown in Photo B. Use a medium-point black paint pen to make dots. Let dry.

6 When all paint is dry, wipe off any remaining pencil with a soft, damp cloth. Spray a light coat of glaze sealer over each tile. It is important that

continued on page 32

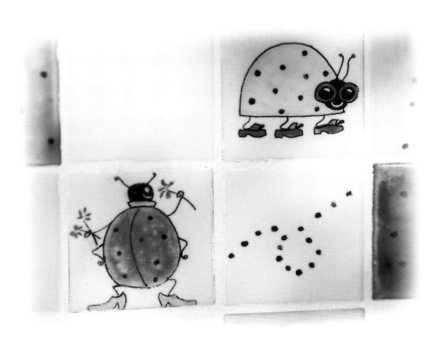

little-lady bug tiles

the first one or two coats of sealer are light. If sprayed on too heavy, the glaze pools on the surface and causes some markers to dissolve and run. Spray several coats, allowing to dry in between. This should be done before applying the tile to the wall surface. If your tile is already grouted onto a surface, it may be easier to use a brush-on glaze sealer rather than a spray. Brush lightly, being careful not to brush back and forth excessively. Let dry.

7 Glue the tile in place according to the tile manufacturer's directions. Let dry. When applying grout, do not apply too liberally. Fill in the crevices well, but avoid the tile surfaces as much as possible. Grout is abrasive and can scratch off paint and sealer. Let the grout dry. Cautiously wipe off tile surfaces with soft, damp cloth. Do not scrub.

Note: To clean tiles, wipe gently with a soft, damp cloth. Do not use an abrasive cleanser.

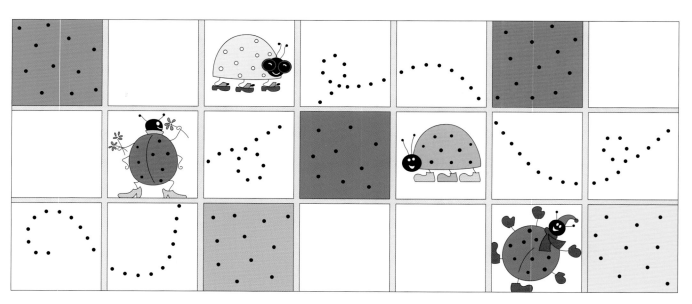

TILE ARRANGEMENT

BUG PATTERNS

PAINTING COLOR GUIDES

smart snack set

SNACK LOVERS WILL RACE TO THE CUPBOARD

FOR THESE HANDSOME POPCORN BOWLS. ADHESIVE

LETTERS MAKE IT EASY TO LABEL THE BOWLS NEATLY,

WHILE METALLIC WAVY LINES ADD A TOUCH OF CLASS.

1 Wash and dry the bowls. Apply adhesive letters to spell BIG BOWL OF POPCORN, creating a curved or flowing line of letters around the bowl. Rub letters with the back of a spoon.

2 Use the masking tape to make a line above and below the words, following the curve created by the words. Burnish the tape with the back of the spoon.

3 Follow the directions on the paint jar and paint black over the letters, keeping the paint between the masking tape lines. Let the paint dry.

4 Remove the tape and letters. The tip of a crafts knife helps to lift off the corners of the letters. Use a paintbrush and black paint to touch up any rough edges. Let dry.

5 Use the wax pencil to lightly draw a wiggly line above and below the black stripe, making the line below larger than the one above. Use gold paint and a brush to paint the wavy line. Let dry. Paint a second coat if necessary. Let dry. Bake the bowl in the oven according to the paint manufacturer's directions.

Ceramic bowls
Adhesive letters (1 inch for large bowl;
   ½ inch for small bowl)
Spoon
¾-inch-wide masking tape
Oven-set porcelain paint in black and gold
Paintbrushes
Crafts knife
Wax pencil

PAINTING PROJECTS TO USE
outdoors

INSTEAD OF BRINGING THE OUTDOORS IN, THIS FUN-FILLED

CHAPTER ENCOURAGES YOUR TALENT TO SPREAD

FROM WITHIN YOUR HOME OUT TO YOUR GLORIOUS YARD.

COME ALONG TO PAINT CHEERY STEPPING-STONES,

MAILBOXES, SWING SEATS, PARK BENCHES,

AND PICNIC TABLES—EVEN GARDEN FEEDERS TO

KEEP FEATHERED FRIENDS HAPPY YEAR-ROUND.

EACH OF THESE OUTDOOR PROJECTS WILL ADD

A DASH OF CHARM TO WELCOME YOU HOME.

TIPS FOR PAINTING PROJECTS
TO USE outdoors

GENERAL TIPS

Painting items to be placed outdoors adds personality to your home's exterior. Whether a garden accessory or a functional table, these pieces can be protected from or enhanced by the weather.

SURFACE PREPARATION

No matter if an item will be used indoors or out, the appropriate preparation must be made for the paint to adhere correctly.

Wood items should be sanded and then wiped clean with a tack cloth. Dirty or dusty pieces should be washed in soapy water and allowed to dry thoroughly. A power washer can be used on large pieces such as a picnic table. Consider taking large pieces to a car wash to clean it before beginning a project. It is always a good idea to apply a coat of sanding sealer to wood pieces before painting. This helps provide a smoother painting surface on the raised wood grain. To use, apply sanding sealer to bare wood using a brush. Let dry. Lightly sand the wood a second time. Wipe away the dust with a tack cloth, and it is ready to paint.

Metal pieces should be washed and dried before painting. If there is rust on a piece, use a rust remover to eliminate those areas. Sand the piece smooth if necessary.

Plastic and terra-cotta pieces should be washed and dried before painting. It is important that any type of surface thoroughly dry before painting or priming.

If the entire surface of an item is going to be painted, it is wise to apply a spray primer first. Choose one that is made specifically for the surface being painted. When using spray paint, be sure to work in a well-ventilated area and avoid breathing in the fumes. Cover all surfaces with newspaper to protect them from paint. A cardboard box works well as a paint box for small items.

TRANSFERRING TIPS

Some of the projects in this chapter require the use of patterns. For more help on transferring patterns, see *page 5*.

When transferring a pattern using a stylus, place a sheet of waxed paper on top of it to help you keep track of lines already traced. The stylus will etch the waxed paper as you work, showing clearly where you've traced.

To remove chalk or transfer paper lines after painting, rub off marks with a soft cloth dampened with clean water. Graphite or other commercial transfer papers may require mineral spirits. Transfer as little of the design as possible to the wood. This will allow you to be more creative with painting.

MIXING PAINTS

If using acrylic paints, mix them together to create a rainbow of colors. If spray-painting a project, apply light coats of different colors to create different hues, texture, and depth.

APPLYING A TOP COAT

If your goal is to achieve a weathered look, do not apply a top coat over the paint. The sun, rain, and other elements will fade and weather away some of the painted design. This look is sometimes desired for a natural or rustic appearance.

If you wish to maintain the painting and hue on a piece, protect it with a spray- or brush-on clear top coat. Choose a varnish, shellac, glaze, sealer, or other clear coat appropriate for the surface and paint used. Follow the manufacturer's instructions. It is usually recommended to apply two to three coats for long-lasting weather protection, and additional coats may be needed as the elements peel off the top layer of sealant.

picnic pizzazz

LET THE WEATHERING SHINE THROUGH

ON THIS SUBTLY PAINTED TABLE.

WATERCOLOR PENCILS AND ACRYLIC PAINTS CREATE

THE SQUARE DESIGNS THAT GRACE THE

TABLE AND BENCH TOPS. VIVID ACRYLICS

GIVE A BURST OF COLOR TO THE LEGS.

WHAT YOU'LL NEED

Weathered picnic table
Medium sandpaper
Tack cloth
Tape measure
Masking tape
Acrylic paints in white, red, orange, purple,
*   turquoise, yellow, and lime green*
Flat paintbrushes
Watercolor pencils in red, yellow, green,
*   turquoise, magenta, and purple*
Water
Spray acrylic sealer

TIPS BEFORE YOU BEGIN

Look for weathered wood furniture at flea markets, secondhand shops, and garage sales. If cleaning is needed, you may want to take the piece to a car wash for a power rinse.

If a piece is stained, mix one part bleach and four parts water to use as cleaner. Follow up with a water rinse. This procedure may eliminate the desired weathered color, so experiment before applying over the entire table. When using bleach, wear protective gloves, eyewear, and old clothes in case of splatters.

instructions continued on page 42

picnic pizzozz

HERE'S HOW

1 Lightly sand all surfaces of the picnic table to remove any extremely rough areas. Remove the dust with a tack cloth.

2 Measure the length and width of one board on the tabletop. The squares will be taped off 1 inch smaller than the width. (For example, if your board is 6 inches wide, the squares will all be 5-inch squares.) Determine how to tape off the squares, leaving 1 inch between each square on a board. Depending on the length of the board, you may need to leave unpainted areas at each end. Tape off the squares on the entire tabletop and on each bench.

A

3 Using very little white acrylic paint, begin painting in the taped-off square areas as shown in Photo A. Use brushstrokes in varying directions, letting some of the wood and grain show through. Let dry. Remove the tape.

4 Using watercolor pencils, color squares and square outlines inside each of the white areas as shown in Photo B. The colored areas can be centered or in one corner as shown in the photo on *page 40*. Use a variety of colors in each white square.

B

5 When all squares are colored, outline each white square with all six watercolor pencils, blending one color into the next. Each outline can be different; just be sure to overlap pencil marks when changing colors.

6 To blend watercolor pencil markings, dip a paintbrush in water and shake off the excess. Paint over the pencil areas, trying to maintain the square shapes in the center as shown in Photo C. Rinse brush often so that the colors stay vibrant. Paint water over the outlines around each white square. Let the paint dry.

7 Use various colors of acrylic paint and a small flat paintbrush to outline each painted design as shown in Photo D. Paint all sides of the legs using acrylic paint, letting the wood and grain show through. Let the paint dry. If a more weathered look is preferred, lightly sand the painted surfaces.

8 Apply two to three coats of spray acrylic sealer to the entire picnic table, letting it dry between coats.

THIS FREEHAND-STYLE PAINTING MAKES FOR
A GOOD FAMILY PROJECT. LET THE KIDS PITCH IN TO PAINT
OR COLOR USING WATERCOLOR PENCILS. YOU'LL
END UP WITH A TABLE OF WHICH YOU CAN ALL BE PROUD.

fanciful feeder

WHAT YOU'LL NEED

*Terra-cotta flowerpot saucers, one each
    of 4-, 6-, 10-, 13-, and two 3-inch
    diameters*
Strong adhesive, such as Liquid Nails
Protective eyewear
Drill; masonry drill bit
Wall texture medium
*Outdoor paints in cream, coral, ocher, orange,
    magenta, and purple*
1½- to 2-inch-wide flat paintbrush
Driftwood; saw
Green-colored wood stain
Fine sandpaper; tack cloth
Drywall screw; screwdriver
Rubber washer
Small ornamental dried gourd
Thin wood scrap; scissors
Small drill bit
Small paintbrush

TIPS BEFORE YOU BEGIN

Be sure to use safety glasses when drilling. Never let a child use an electric tool
unless supervised.

If gourds are not available in your area, use the Internet to find sources for ordering them.
You can purchase them dried and cleaned, which will save you time.

instructions continued on page 46

THIS NATURAL-LOOKING FEEDER WILL ADD A
RUSTIC TOUCH TO YOUR GARDEN AS WELL AS
FEED THE BIRDS. THE COMBINATION OF SURFACE
TEXTURES—TERRA-COTTA, DRIFTWOOD, AND A GOURD—
MAKES FOR AN INTERESTING MIX, READY TO BE
ENHANCED WITH PAINT AND STAIN.

fanciful feeder

HERE'S HOW

1 Gather saucers together. Set aside the largest saucer to be used for the base and one 3-inch saucer for the top. Stack the remaining saucers from largest to smallest. Glue together with a generous amount of adhesive as shown in Photo A. Let dry.

2 Put on protective eyewear. To prepare the base saucer, drill several holes in the base. Drill one in the center to insert a screw. Drill at least two others for drainage holes.

3 Mix wall texture with cream- colored paint, mixing about one part texture to four parts paint. Paint all exposed surfaces of all saucers as shown in Photo B, filling the crevices generously. Let dry. If more texture is desired, paint another coat. Let dry.

4 Use coral, ocher, orange, magenta, and purple to paint terra-cotta pieces. Thin the paint with water so it is thin enough to run and looks transparent. Use a wide flat paintbrush and brush on sections of color, allowing the paint to run and blend together as shown in Photo C. If stronger color is desired, paint on more coats, allowing to dry between coats.

A

B

STACKING FLOWERPOT SAUCERS ALLOWS YOU TO MAKE
THIS ATTRACTIVE FEEDER ANY DESIRED SIZE. COVERING
THEM WITH WALL TEXTURE ADDS A SANDY TOP COAT.

46

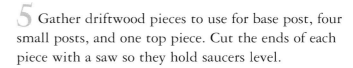

5 Gather driftwood pieces to use for base post, four small posts, and one top piece. Cut the ends of each piece with a saw so they hold saucers level.

6 Brush the green-colored wood stain onto the wood as shown in Photo D. Let the stain soak in. When dry, sand the driftwood. Sand just enough to enhance the wood grain. Wipe dust off with a tack cloth.

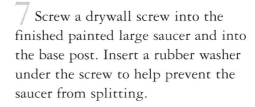

7 Screw a drywall screw into the finished painted large saucer and into the base post. Insert a rubber washer under the screw to help prevent the saucer from splitting.

8 Use adhesive to glue the four posts to the base saucer. Let dry. Place a generous amount of glue on tops of posts and set stack of saucers on top. Let dry.

9 Glue the top driftwood piece to the top saucer. Let dry.

10 To make the bird, use a small ornamental gourd that is cured and dried. Clean gourd if necessary. Use a thin slice of wood and scissors to cut a triangular tail shape and another sliver for the beak. Drill a hole in the gourd and insert the beak. Use a small drill bit to drill a line of holes and insert the tail. Stain the bird with green stain. Let dry. Dot two coral-colored eyes using the handle of a paintbrush. Glue bird on the last saucer and let dry. Glue saucer on the top driftwood piece. Let dry.

brick beauty

DOT THE GARDEN WITH COLORFUL BRICKS FOR
AN UNEXPECTED SURPRISE. PUT THESE BEAUTIES
END TO END TO MAKE AN EDGING, OR PLACE THEM
TOGETHER TO FORM LARGER SQUARE OR
RECTANGULAR STEPPING-STONES.

WHAT YOU'LL NEED

Decorative brick
Newspapers
White spray primer
Acrylic paints for outdoor use in white, red,
  purple, yellow, green, and orange
Medium round and fine liner paintbrushes
Tracing paper
Pencil with soft lead
Tape
Fine-point black paint pen

HERE'S HOW

1 Wash and dry the brick. In a well-ventilated work area, cover the work surface with newspapers. Spray the brick with white primer. Let dry.

2 Paint the top of the brick white. Let dry. Paint the sides red. Let dry.

3 Trace full-size pattern, *page 50,* onto tracing paper and color back of tracing with soft lead pencil. Tape paper onto brick, right side up. Draw over outline with very sharp pencil as shown in Photo A, transferring the pattern. If the brick is too rough to transfer the pattern, cut out patterns and trace around them.

4 Using the color pattern on *page 51* as a guide, paint in the designs. Use a fine liner brush to paint in green vines. Paint purple vertical stripes over the red on the sides of the brick. Let dry.

5 Use a black paint pen to outline the designs as shown in Photo B. Draw a zigzag border around the yellow.

6 On the large flower, make a black dot on each point. To paint dots, dip the handle of a large paintbrush in paint and dot onto surface. Let dry. Use a smaller paintbrush handle to add yellow dots in the center of the black dots. Let dry.

BRICK PATTERN

BRICK PAINTING GUIDE

sentimental seating

THIS ROMANTIC PARK BENCH COMBINES

WOODBURNING AND PAINTING FOR A STUNNING APPEARANCE.

USE THE PATTERN ON PAGE 55, OR PERSONALIZE

THE BENCH WITH SENTIMENTAL DESIGNS OF YOUR OWN.

TIPS BEFORE YOU BEGIN

Benches like this one can be purchased unfinished at home centers, discount stores, antique stores, and flea markets.

If you find a painted one, use stripper to remove the paint, and clean the wood slats thoroughly.

When choosing the bench, look for one in which the wood slats are screwed in place. Remove the slats before beginning for ease of woodburning and painting.

Because this project uses oil paints, be sure to leave ample time for drying. Acrylics can be used with a clear top coat, but oil paint blends especially nicely when painting in this style.

WHAT YOU'LL NEED

Park bench with unfinished or lightly varnished wood
Sandpaper
Tack cloth
Screwdriver
Newspapers
Pencil
Tracing paper
Scissors
Wood-burning tool
Oil paints in magenta, purple, red, blue, green, yellow, and white
Glass or hard plate
Medium flat paintbrush
Oil-painting medium, such as linseed oil
Clear sealer or varnish

instructions continued on page 54

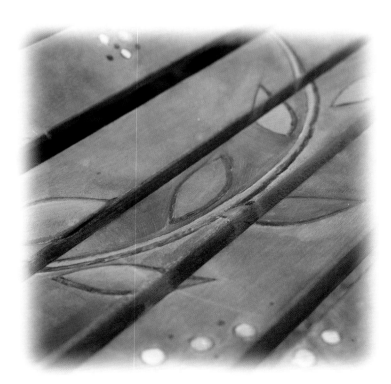

sentimental seating

HERE'S HOW

1 Purchase a park bench in light- or medium-colored wood, preferably with little or no finish on it. Sand each piece of wood to remove most of the sealer finish. Wipe off dust using a tack cloth.

2 Use a screwdriver to remove the slats from the bench. Cover the work surface with newspapers. Lay the slats on the work surface in the order they attach to the bench. Make sure they are laid down in proper order with top sides up. Refer to your assembly instructions. Lay the pieces down butted together with edges aligned.

3 Use a pencil to draw a heart, initials, a vine, or other favorite motifs. If desired, trace the leaf and vine pattern, *opposite,* to use as a design. Cut out the pattern and lay it on the wood. Trace around the pattern.

4 Use a wood-burning tool to burn around penciled outline as shown in Photo A, creating a defined dark line.

5 Arrange oil paints onto a glass or other hard plate (not foam).

6 Work on the background first. Using a medium flat paintbrush, brush small dabs of paint onto wood. Use an oil-painting medium to thin paint. Place a quarter-size dab of oil-painting medium on plate, dip brush in it, and blend into paint. This will thin the paint and help to spread it and work it into the wood like a stain. Blend the colors together—blue to purple, purple to magenta, magenta to red—as shown in photo B. Add bits of white where you want to lighten the color.

LEAF AND VINE PATTERN   **1 SQUARE = 1 INCH**

7 For the green leaves, start with green and blend into a yellow as shown in Photo C. Add a bit of white to highlight. Paint the heart in the same manner, using magenta and red and highlighting with white. Spread the wood slats apart enough to paint the edges. Assemble onto the metal frame. Paint the back of slats. The bench may take several days or weeks to dry, depending on the thickness of paint used and the humidity.

8 When completely dry, use a clear sealer or varnish meant for use outdoors. Paint on one or two coats, allowing to dry between coats.

swing sensation

WHAT YOU'LL NEED

Purchased plastic swing seats
*   or 9×22-inch piece of*
*   1½-inch-thick wood*
Drill with ½-inch bit
Fine sandpaper
Tack cloth
Newspapers; tracing paper; pencil
Clear sanding sealer for wood seats or white
*   spray primer paint for plastic seats*
Transfer paper
Oil paints in white, cerulean blue, red, naples
*   yellow, and burnt umber*
½- and ¼-inch-wide flat oil paintbrushes
Turpentine

TIPS BEFORE YOU BEGIN

You may wish to purchase lightweight plastic swing seats. For young children, plastic swing seats are safer than heavy wood seats.

If using plastic seats, you may need to adjust the size of the patterns on the following pages to fit the seats.

Be sure to check the weight limitations of the rope you select to hold the seats. Also make sure it is properly secured to avoid injury. For more support, drill two holes on each side of the swing seat.

instructions continued on page 58

ENJOY THE CAREFREE DAYS OF SUMMER
SWINGING THROUGH THE AIR ON A SEAT YOU PAINTED
USING ANY OF THESE FUN DESIGNS.

57

swing sensation

A

HERE'S HOW

1 If using wood seats, mark and drill a pair of holes in each swing seat as indicated on the pattern, *pages 60–61*. Sand the swing seat surfaces and remove the dust with a tack cloth. Prime the wood using a clear sanding sealer. Let dry. Sand lightly and remove dust. If using plastic seats, lightly sand the surfaces and remove the dust with a tack cloth. In a well-ventilated work area, cover the work surface with newspapers. Spray the seat with primer. Let dry.

2 Enlarge the desired pattern, *pages 60–61,* to fit the swing seat top. Trace the pattern onto tracing paper. It is not necessary to trace the lettering. Place transfer paper, right side down, on the swing seat top. Place the pattern on top of the transfer paper. Retrace the lines of the pattern as shown in Photo A, pressing firmly. Remove the transfer paper and the pattern.

3 Using burnt umber, paint over each of the traced lines as shown in Photo B. Continue the lines down the sides of the swing seat as needed.

B

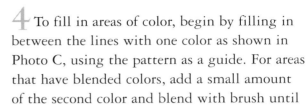

4 To fill in areas of color, begin by filling in between the lines with one color as shown in Photo C, using the pattern as a guide. For areas that have blended colors, add a small amount of the second color and blend with brush until the desired look is achieved as shown in Photo D. Clean the brush with turpentine as needed.

5 With no paint on the paintbrush, begin to blend the burnt umber lines with the color that is butting against it. To blend the colors, make small brushstrokes in the direction of the burnt umber lines, blending the colors slightly at the edges of the outline. Clean the brush with turpentine as often as needed.

6 When all painting is complete, add the lettering as shown on the desired pattern. Place the swing seat in a dry, warm place to dry. This may take several days or even weeks.

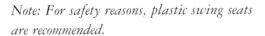

Note: For safety reasons, plastic swing seats are recommended.

THE SKY'S THE LIMIT! SWING SEAT PATTERN

1 SQUARE = 1 INCH

UP, UP, AND AWAY! SWING SEAT PATTERN 1 SQUARE = 1 INCH

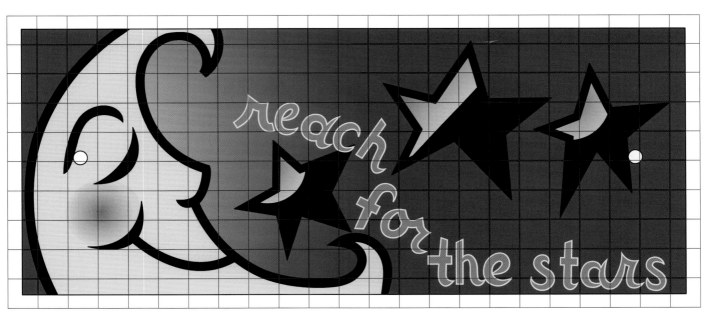

REACH FOR THE STARS SWING SEAT PATTERN 1 SQUARE = 1 INCH

lovely letter box

YOU'LL MAKE THE LETTER CARRIER SMILE
WITH THIS CHARMING HEART-LADEN BOX AWAITING
EACH DAY'S DELIVERY.

Metal mailbox; tools for assembly
White spray primer
Newspapers; Disposable plate
Acrylic paints in orange, pink, purple, and
     pale butter yellow
Sponge and water
Tracing paper; pencil
Scissors
Gold marker pen; 2 wood hearts; paintbrush
Strong adhesive, such as E6000
Spray acrylic sealer

HERE'S HOW

1 Before assembling the mailbox, prime it with white spray primer. In a well-ventilated work area, cover the work surface with newspapers. Spray an even coat of primer over each of the mailbox pieces. Do this step even if your mailbox is already white. Let dry. Spray a second coat if needed. Let dry.

2 Arrange small quarter-size dabs of paint onto plate. Soak a sponge in water. Squeeze out the excess and begin dabbing paint onto mailbox using all colors as shown in Photo A. Gently blend one color into another. Don't over-sponge the colors. Paint all pieces, including the flag and handle. Paint the inside of the lid and as far inside the mailbox as desired. Let dry.

3 Trace the full-size heart patterns, *pages 64–65,* onto tracing paper. Cut out and randomly trace onto mailbox. Draw in heart shapes with gold marker pen as shown in Photo B. Fill in the hearts with stripes, swirls, plaid, and other desired patterns. Let dry.

4 Assemble the mailbox. If the mailbox has a plastic flag, cut the flag portion off the stem with sharp scissors. Paint two wood hearts purple. Let dry. Add decoration with gold pen. Glue the hearts to the flag stem. In a well-ventilated work area, spray mailbox with sealer. Let dry.

5 Mount the mailbox to a post. If desired, paint the post to coordinate with the mailbox.

LETTER BOX PATTERNS

PAINTING
flea market finds

THE THRILL OF THE HUNT IS HALF THE FUN OF

TURNING FLEA MARKET FINDS INTO PERSONALIZED

TREASURES. IN THIS EXCITING CHAPTER, LEARN

HOW TO TRANSFORM CHAIRS, DISPLAY CASES,

LUNCH BOXES, TRAYS—EVEN CASTAWAY TELEVISIONS—

INTO ONE-OF-A-KIND PIECES YOU'LL USE AND

DISPLAY WITH PRIDE. ALL IT TAKES IS YOUR

PERSONAL CREATIVITY AND A PALETTE FULL OF PAINT.

TIPS FOR PAINTING
flea market finds

GENERAL TIPS

If you haven't been bitten by the flea market bug yet, get ready! In this chapter you'll get wonderful ideas for specific flea market projects. You'll also learn to look at objects with an artful eye. This adds another layer to your creative endeavors and makes working on a project just that much more fun.

WHAT ARE FLEA MARKET FINDS?

Flea market finds are items that can be given a new life with your creative touch. You may have items right at home—in a garage, attic, or basement—that simply need a facelift. Other good places to find castaway items are garage sales, secondhand shops, estate sales, flea markets, antique shops, and furniture store bargain areas.

WHAT TO LOOK FOR

Look for items that are in good structural shape and have a use, such as a chair or table. When you find an item that has an interesting shape or intrigues you, explore the possibilities for ways to use the item. A good example is the box on *page 78*. This one stores paint bottles, but a lunch box can also be used to store doll clothes, a postcard collection, or any number of small items. While you may decide to paint a piece simply as an art object, if it can be used for a purpose, all the better.

PREPARING TO SHOP

The hunt for flea market objects is a fun outing by yourself, with friends, or with the entire family. Make a list before you go shopping if you're looking for particular items, jotting down sizes if necessary. One tip: Never buy an item without knowing what you'll use it for. Otherwise you'll find yourself putting these "treasures" right back in your own garage sale.

Things to take along on your shopping spree include a tape measure, a pencil, and paper. If

that need repair. Be sure you're up to the task and that the costs won't exceed your spending limitations. You may also have to sand, remove rust, or scrub an item before paint can be applied properly. Keep these things in mind when choosing your items to be painted.

FLEA MARKET DECORATING

Because a mix-and-match decorating scheme adds warmth and personality to a home, painting flea market finds fits right in today's look. So keep your options open and enjoy the hunt—it's half the fun of creating a one-of-a-kind work of art. You'll be surprised at how you'll start to look at "lovingly used" furniture and other items from a brand-new point of view.

unsure about an item, inquire if it can be held for a certain amount of time. Most places, such as flea markets, garage sales, and secondhand shops, will have an "all sales are final" policy, so make wise buying decisions.

TRANSFORMING FLEA MARKET FINDS WITH PAINT

Keep your eye out for unusual pieces that would come alive with paint. Most castaway items come with a fairly inexpensive price tag, so you don't have to spend a lot of money on your painting "canvas." But you could have a masterpiece in the end.

PAINTING PREPARATION

There are a couple of drawbacks when it comes to painting flea market finds. The preparation may be more of a chore than you want to tackle. For instance, if a piece is painted and you want to strip it, that takes time, money, and patience. To have it professionally done may be worth the expense, depending on your budget and the intricacy of the piece. You may also find things

chair charm

WHAT YOU'LL NEED

Chair with wide center and top
 back supports
Screwdriver, optional
Fine sandpaper
Tack cloth
Acrylic paint in pink, blue, and ivory
Medium and large flat paintbrushes
Stencil cream in mauve and country blue
Stencil paintbrush
Tracing paper; pencil
Tape
Fine liner paintbrush
Clear acrylic sealer

TIPS BEFORE
YOU BEGIN

If possible, disassemble the chair before beginning the project. This will enable you to easily lay down the chair back down for painting. It also will help you avoid getting paint splatters on areas where you don't want them, such as the hardware or upholstery.

If necessary, strip the original paint from all surfaces. Sand all surfaces smooth and wipe away the dust with a tack cloth. Apply a sanding sealer, let dry, and sand again. This will prepare the chair so the new paint will adhere properly.

Once the chair is painted, consider having the seat reupholstered. If desired, use a plain canvas fabric and paint it to match the chair using fabric paint.

instructions continued on page 72

BEFORE

EVEN WITH ITS SANDED EDGES, THIS SUBTLY

SHADED CHAIR HAS AN ELEGANT FLAIR

BECAUSE OF THE CHAIR SHAPE AND THE PAINT COLOR

SELECTION. USE THE PATTERNS ON PAGES 74-75

OR ADAPT THEM TO FIT YOUR PARTICULAR CHAIR.

chair charm

A

HERE'S HOW

1 If necessary, remove the upholstered seat with a screwdriver before beginning.

2 Wash and dry the chair surfaces. Sand the surfaces to remove any glossy sheen from the surface. Wipe off dust with a tack cloth.

3 Lay the chair down to avoid having the paint run. On this chair it was easiest to paint the design upside down so the chair seat was not in the way. Decide which areas you want to remain pink and blue, such as on the chair base and round details (see photo on *page 70*). Paint those areas first.

4 Using a medium flat brush, paint the remainder of the chair pink. Let dry. Paint over the pink area with blue as shown in Photo A. Let dry. Paint over the blue area with ivory. Avoid the pink and blue detailed areas. Let the paint dry.

5 Sand the surfaces until the desired effect is achieved as shown in Photo B. Sand all surfaces, a little more on the edges. Sand until the different layers of pink and blue paint and bare wood appear in certain spots. Wipe off dust with a tack cloth.

B

6 Choose areas to shade in with mauve and blue. Use mauve and blue stencil cream and a stencil brush. Begin in a corner or at an edge as shown in Photo C. Apply a small amount of cream along the edge and blend outward to get a soft, faded cloud of color. Also apply color to various areas where the design will go. Use very little paint to achieve a soft, subtle look. Add another layer if desired. Let dry.

7 Trace the patterns, *pages 74–75*, onto tracing paper. Use a soft pencil to color the back of pattern. Tape the pattern onto the chair, centering each design over the appropriate back piece. Using a sharp pencil, trace the pattern outlines as shown in Photo D. Remove the pattern.

8 Using a fine liner paintbrush, paint in the design with ivory paint. Paint a second coat if needed. Let dry. Add a blue shadow over the ivory design as shown in Photo E. Let dry. In a well-ventilated work area, spray the chair with clear sealer. Let dry.

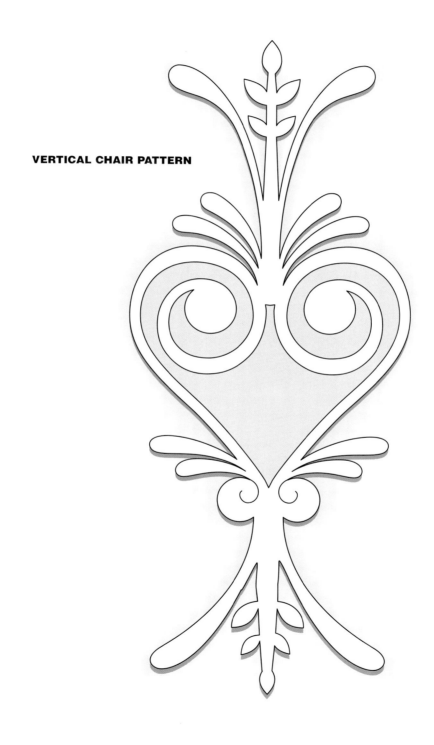

VERTICAL CHAIR PATTERN

TOP

HORIZONTAL CHAIR PATTERN

delightful display

BRIGHT ENAMEL PAINTS ADD PIZZAZZ
TO THIS ONCE ORDINARY DISPLAY CABINET.

HERE'S HOW

1 Remove any hardware from the cabinet with a screwdriver. Sand all surfaces of the cabinet. Wipe off the dust using a tack cloth.

2 Before painting, mask off glass areas and any area you do not wish to paint. Use wide masking tape and tape tightly along edges. Tape newspapers over large areas.

3 In a well-ventilated work area, cover the work surface with newspapers. Spray a coat of primer on the cabinet and let dry. It may take several coats until the surface is almost completely covered. Let dry between coats. Do not remove the masking tape.

4 Paint largest areas first. Paint the white areas using at least a 2-inch-wide flat paintbrush. You can overlap into colored areas that will be painted later.

5 Use a small flat paintbrush for painting in colored areas. Use the grooves, sections, and detail shapes as a guide for breaking up blocks of color. Paint in largest sections first, overlapping into other areas as needed. Cover up the overlaps with the next color. Use a fine liner paintbrush to make thin stripes. Do not try to make them perfect. Paint in checks with a narrow flat brush. To make dots, dip the handle of a paintbrush in paint and dot onto the surface. Let the paint dry.

6 Paint the stars separately. Paint the edges a contrasting color. Layer and glue stars in sets of two. When dry, glue the stars onto finished painted cabinet. Let dry.

7 Paint wood knobs black and let them dry. Add white swirls and polka dots. Let the paint dry.

8 Remove the masking tape and clean the glass. Put the doors and hardware back in place.

WHAT YOU'LL NEED

China cabinet with straight lines and details
Screwdriver; medium-grade sandpaper
Tack cloth; wide masking tape
Newspapers; white spray primer
Enamel paints in white, red, hot pink, purple,
  lime green, turquoise, yellow, orange, and black
2-inch-wide flat, fine liner, and assorted small
  and medium round paintbrushes
Assorted wood stars
Wood glue; desired wood knobs

BEFORE

art-filled caddy

THIS OLD LUNCH BOX IS GIVEN NEW LIFE

AS AN ART SUPPLY CADDY. FOR TEXTURE, A VARIETY

OF HARDWARE WASHERS WERE ADDED TO THE SURFACE AND

THEN HIGHLIGHTED WITH METALLIC PAINTS.

Metal lunch box
Variety of washers (available in the hardware
    and plumbing sections of home improvement,
    discount, and hardware stores)
Strong adhesive, such as E6000; newspapers
Spray primer paint; silver spray paint
Acrylic paints in silver and other desired
    metallic colors
Small round paintbrush; clear acrylic sealer

HERE'S HOW

I Decide on the
arrangement of washers
on the lunch box. As
shown, *opposite,* you can
place some inside others.
If necessary, cut rubber
washers to fit the edges of the lunch box.
Glue the washers in place as shown in
Photo A. Let dry.

2 In a well-ventilated work area, cover
the surface with newspapers. Open the
lunch box lid and spray the inside with
primer. Let dry. Prop the lid open slightly
and spray primer on the outside of the
lunch box. Let dry. Repeat on the inside
and outside with silver paint. Let dry.

3 Paint the background surfaces where
desired using a metallic paint color. For
example, paint the bottom of the front, the
sides, the handle, and some of the
hardware. After a color is applied, brush
over lightly using silver acrylic paint.

4 Paint the washers using a variety of
metallic colors as shown in Photo B. Let the paint dry.

5 In a well-ventilated work area, cover the surface with
newspapers. Open the lunch box and spray the inside with sealer.
Let dry. Prop the lid open slightly and spray the exterior with
sealer. Let dry.

BEFORE

79

fantastic '50s tv

DON'T TOSS OUT THAT OLD TELEVISION!
BLANKET IT WITH VIVID COLORS AND MOTIFS THAT
SALUTE POPULAR 1950S PATTERNS.

Old television sets have personalities all their own. Use the lines and details of the television as guides for painting.

You may want to take off knobs and remove the screen for ease in painting. If more knobs are desired, check the wood area of a crafts store. Use a strong wood glue or screws to hold knobs in place.

For the screen, you may wish to have an old family photo enlarged, in black and white of course, to insert into the screen.

The artist who painted this television studied '50s fabrics and incorporated some of those patterns. Consult the library for more motifs and colors indicative of the time period.

instructions continued on page 82

WHAT YOU'LL NEED

Cabinet-style television
Sandpaper; tack cloth
Screwdriver; masking tape and paper
Newspapers
White spray primer, such as Kilz
Acrylic paints in black, coral, red,
  turquoise, and yellow
2-inch-wide flat, 3-inch-wide chip (thinly
  bristled and tapered paintbrush, found in
  hardware and home center stores by the
  house painting
  brushes or in crafts
  stores), medium
  round, medium
  flat, and fine liner
  paintbrushes
Copper glaze
Rubber comb
  (available in crafts
  and paint stores)
Medium-point black
  paint pen
Wood knobs, optional
Black-and-white
  photograph or photocopy to
  fit television screen

BEFORE

HERE'S HOW

1 This television set had some rough surfaces, and the finish was cracked and checked. If your TV is similar, sand the surfaces until smooth as shown in Photo A. Wipe off dust with a tack cloth.

2 If possible, remove the glass for ease in painting the wood cabinet. Mask off the screen area with tape and paper.

3 In a well-ventilated work area, cover the work surface with newspapers. Spray the entire surface with a white primer. Let dry. Spray on a second coat if needed. Let dry.

4 Paint the top and the sides of the television black. Let dry.

5 Use a 3-inch-wide chip brush to paint on copper glaze as shown in Photo B. Do this in sections so that you have time to comb the area and make the bean shapes in Step 6 before the glaze dries. Paint the glaze on generously enough to cover the black but still go on smoothly and evenly. Comb through the glaze with a rubber comb using smooth, even strokes as shown in Photo C.

A

B

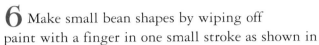

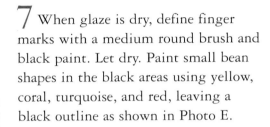

6 Make small bean shapes by wiping off paint with a finger in one small stroke as shown in Photo D. Complete the rest of the surfaces in sections.

7 When glaze is dry, define finger marks with a medium round brush and black paint. Let dry. Paint small bean shapes in the black areas using yellow, coral, turquoise, and red, leaving a black outline as shown in Photo E.

8 Paint remaining television sections red, yellow, turquoise, copper glaze, coral, and black. Let dry. Add large red polka dots on the yellow if desired. Let dry. Make black starburst shapes over the polka dots using a fine liner brush. Let dry.

9 Draw curlicues and flower shapes loosely with a medium-point black paint pen as pictured on *page 81* on the coral area. Let dry.

IO If desired, prime and paint wood knobs to replace the original knobs. Let dry.

II Insert the photo or photocopy inside the television before reattaching the screen.

mad-for-plaid table

TIPS BEFORE YOU BEGIN

The fun part about this project is that it is quick and the outcome is striking. Because you're painting only the tabletop, you can change the color combination fairly easily whenever you wish to change your decor.

When selecting the table, keep in mind that one with a flat top and straight edges is easiest to work with. Avoid round or oval tables.

BEFORE

WHAT YOU'LL NEED

Table with flat, even top
Sandpaper
Tack cloth
Acrylic or latex paint in cream, seafoam green,
*   light purple, and dark teal (or four other*
*   desired colors)*
Medium paintbrush
Yardstick and pencil
Foam paint rollers in 1- and 2-inch widths
Acrylic sealer, optional

instructions continued on page 86

FOAM PAINT ROLLERS MAKE THIS TABLETOP AS EASY
AS ONE-TWO-THREE. USE THE POPULAR COLOR COMBINATION
SHOWN, OR CHOOSE FOUR OTHER COLORS TO
COORDINATE WITH YOUR HOME'S DECORATING SCHEME.

mad-for-plaid table

A

HERE'S HOW

1 Wash and dry the tabletop. Sand any rough edges. Wipe off the dust with a tack cloth. If desired, refinish the legs of the table and varnish them.

2 Paint the top of the table with the cream paint using a paintbrush. Apply a second coat if necessary. Let dry.

3 Using a yardstick and pencil, divide the table into thirds or other desired widths, and make a tiny mark at the side and along a line across the table to serve as a guide as shown in Photo A.

4 Referring to Diagram 1, paint two or three seafoam green stripes across the table using the 2-inch roller as shown in Photo B. Let the paint dry. Mark the table as before to indicate where lines will intersect across the first green lines, dividing the area as desired.

5 Using a 2-inch roller, paint light purple lines over the green lines as shown in Photo C and Diagram 2. Let dry.

6 Mark the table once again, this time crossing the purple lines with green and then purple as shown in Diagrams 3 and 4. Let dry.

7 Using a 1-inch roller and the dark teal paint, repeat with more lines as desired. (See Diagram 5.) Allow the paint to dry. Seal with an acrylic sealer, if desired.

INTERSECTING LINES ADD FASHIONABLE PLAID TO AN ORDINARY TABLETOP. USE THE HELPFUL DIAGRAMS, OPPOSITE, TO RE-CREATE THE LOOK.

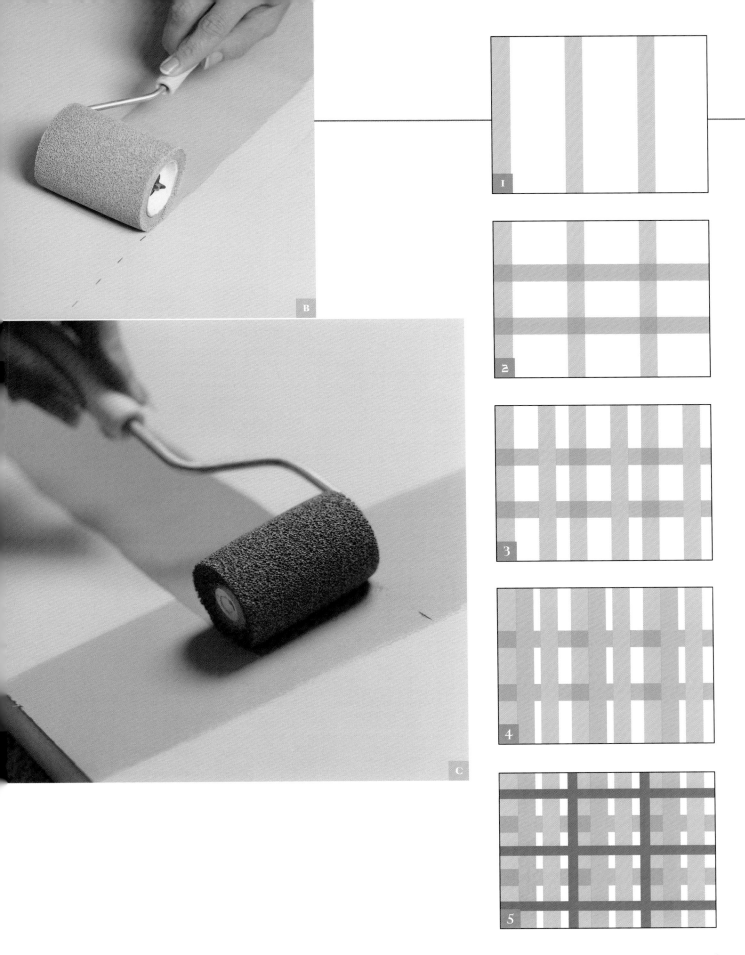

PAINTING ON unusual surfaces

CHALLENGE YOUR PAINTING TALENT BY
EXPANDING YOUR CANVASES TO INCLUDE
UNCONVENTIONAL ITEMS, SUCH AS SHELLS, CORN, GOURDS,
ROCKS, AND MORE. YOU'LL FIND THAT DIMENSIONAL
ITEMS LIKE THESE ARE INSPIRATIONAL
AND PROVIDE WONDERFUL SURFACES TO ENHANCE
WITH A VARIETY OF PAINTING TECHNIQUES.

TIPS FOR PAINTING ON
unusual surfaces

GENERAL TIPS

Painting on unusual surfaces sometimes camouflages the item, while other times it enhances its shape and texture.

You will notice that the items selected as samples in this chapter have unique shapes with interesting textures. Adding paint to these items gives them an element of surprise that makes them unique and appealing.

SELECTING PAINTS

When selecting paints for a project, you must consider the surface to be painted, the use for the item, and whether it will be placed indoors or out. All the projects in this chapter are intended to be placed indoors, so remember to apply a clear outdoor sealer to protect an item from the elements if displaying it outside.

PAINTING NATURAL ITEMS

Be sure that any natural item is cleaned and dried thoroughly before painting. If the item has any moisture in it, it will eventually mold, and the paint will wrinkle and flake off.

In particular, beach items, such as shells and driftwood, should be cleaned thoroughly before painting. If sand is on the surface, either the paint will fall off or the surface will become bumpy.

If you wish to paint shells, you can usually find them in crafts supply stores. If picking up shells on a beach, be sure to check local regulations before removing them.

WHAT CAN BE PAINTED

Nearly everything can be painted as long as it is dry and free of dust, dirt, grease, and rust. If an item is very porous, you may want to apply a sealer to the surface before painting. A slick surface should be lightly sanded, and then a sanding sealer should be applied.

Metal, glass, and plastic surfaces may need special primers before decorative paint is applied. These can often be found in both brush-on and spray-on applications. Depending on the size of your project and the work area you have, one may be preferred over the other. Be sure to let primer dry thoroughly before beginning to paint.

Some surfaces soak up paint more than others. When possible, experiment with a surface before beginning a project to get a feel for the paint application and the brushes that work best for you.

Depending on the use of the project and where it will be (indoors or out), you may want to apply a top coat to the piece. Many sealers are available today in a variety of sheens. When making a selection, just be sure it is compatible with the paint used.

EXPANDING YOUR CANVAS

Whether shopping or hiking, keep your eyes open for interesting items to paint. Sometimes it helps to look at items as art objects in themselves. For instance, consider an oversized wood spoon. While it may not be functional or very attractive as is, think of it painted with colors and motifs that coordinate with your kitchen. Suddenly it could be a one-of-a-kind towel rack.

Check out farmers markets or grocery stores for stalks of corn. Consider the size desired when selecting the corn. Indian corn can also be used.

For the bug pin, check out flea markets for fun gem-embellished bugs. Any color of pin will work with this project, the wilder the better.

We've used beaded wire from a craft store as spiral accents. If beaded wire is not available, thread desired beads onto 10-inch lengths of 24-gauge wire as an alternative. Make small loops in the wire ends to hold the beads in place.

instructions continued on page 94

Ear of corn on stalk; sharp knife
Gold acrylic paint in bottle
Paintbrush
Newspapers
Spray paint in deep red, purple, and aqua blue; paper; tape
3 pieces of iridescent clear beaded wire
Hot-glue gun; glue sticks
Bug jewelry

IMAGINE THESE PRETTY EARS OF CORN

GRACING THE TABLE AT THANKSGIVING. THE INSTRUCTIONS

USE SOFT METALLIC TONES, BUT THESE HUSKS

COULD HAVE BRIGHT COATS OF PAINT FOR AN

EVEN MORE CONTEMPORARY LOOK.

A

HERE'S HOW

1 Choose a firm stalk of corn with stalk itself still intact. Cut to length desired. Carefully peel back shucks without tearing them off corn. Peel back until the corn is well exposed. Remove the silk threads.

2 Paint the kernels a gold color as shown in Photo A. Let dry. Paint another coat if needed. Let dry.

3 Wrap paper around the corn and tape it in place to protect it while painting the shucks. In a well-ventilated work area, lay the opened corn on newspapers. Spread the shucks as far away from the corn as possible. Spray portions of the shucks blue as shown in Photo B. Let dry. Next add some purple overlapping the blue in some areas but not completely covering the blue as shown in Photo C.

B

4 Remove the paper. Add red, overlapping some onto the blue and purple and allowing those colors to show through as in Photo D. Allow the red paint to overspray onto the corn. Spray and overlap each color so that the end result shows a deep red that blends into a purple that blends into an blue. Let dry.

5 Coil the ends of three pieces of beaded wire. Hot-glue the uncoiled ends between the corn and the shucks. Hot-glue bug pin onto the kernels.

A BLENDING OF SPRAY PAINTS ADDS INTEREST
TO THE SHUCKS OF THIS EAR OF CORN. THE BEADED TENDRILS
AND BEJEWELED BUG ADD SPARKLING FOCAL POINTS.

shimmering shells

IRIDESCENT PAINTS ON TINY SEASHELLS

ADD COLOR AND SPARKLE.

APPLY THEM AROUND THE EDGE OF A SAND-COVERED BOWL,

AND THEY LOOK AS IF IN THEIR NATURAL SETTING.

Shells; waxed paper
Iridescent paints in white, hot pink, purple,
*   turquoise, yellow, and lime green*
Disposable plate
Small and medium flat paint brushes
Fine white glitter
Several cups of white sand
Decoupage medium; glass bowl
Thick white crafts glue; candles

HERE'S HOW

1 Wash and dry shells. Cover work surface with waxed paper.

2 Place a small amount of each paint color on a disposable plate. You will use mostly iridescent white. Paint the entire shell iridescent white. While wet, add a touch of color to the painted shell. A tiny bit of intense color goes a long way on the white. Dip the tip of a brush into color and paint onto the shell. While still wet, clean brush and add another color in another area; subtly blend the colors together. Experiment with color combinations, such as pink and yellow, yellow and green, green and turquoise, turquoise and purple, and purple and pink. Add a third color or just paint solid. Let shells dry.

3 Mix about ½ teaspoon of fine white glitter into ½ cup of white sand.

4 To decorate the glass bowl, paint the outside with a thick, even coat of decoupage medium. Using glue, glue some shells onto the side. Pour the glitter-sand mixture onto wet decoupage medium, and pour off excess. Repeat this process until covered. Let dry. To keep the sand in place, handle the bowl from the inside or the bottom.

5 Glue shells around the top rim. Let dry.

6 Fill the bowl with sand, sprinkle a little glitter on top, and insert candles in the center.

Note: Never leave burning candles unattended.

king humpty

MAKE SURE THIS HUMPTY SITS UP STRAIGHT SO HE
DOESN'T TOPPLE FROM THE WALL. MADE FROM A
LARGE GOURD, HE IS A CHARMING FELLOW INDEED.

Begin with a hard, cured gourd such as this martin house gourd of the bottle type gourd family. It is about 12 inches wide and 15 inches high with the stem intact.

No two gourds will be alike. Some may be wider, rounder, taller, symmetrical or oddly shaped. They will each develop their own character as they are transformed into Humpty.

Gourds can be grown or purchased in the fall when harvested. Check that the gourd seems solid and not too lightweight, with no weak or thin spots. The shell of this gourd is about ¼ inch thick. Thin shells can crack very easily during the creating process.

Gourds are often green or ivory in color when freshly picked. They need ample time to dry and cure to become hard and acquire a nice wood tone color. They will often mold and look terrible in the curing process. Unless they have become soft, this is a natural process and will not harm the gourd. If the gourd is soft, it is rotten and cannot be used. The drying process can take weeks or months. If you are drying the gourd yourself, allow it to sit in a warm, dry environment. When cured, it should feel like hard wood and sound and feel hollow. You may even be able to hear the seeds rattle inside.

Clean the gourd with warm soapy water and a plastic scrubber. It may help to soak the gourd to soften the skin. There may be patches of skin and probably mold that are black and/or white. Some of the skin patches can be difficult to remove. Hold the blade of a sharp knife at an angle to scrape these patches, keeping wet while you work. After cleaning it, thoroughly dry it. It should have a smooth, warm brown surface and possibly some mottled coloring.

instructions continued on page 100

WHAT YOU'LL NEED

Hard, cured large gourd; scraper
Sharp nonserrated knife; towel
1-inch hole saw bit and drill; wood glue
Fine-tooth handsaw; paintbrush
Wood stain; rag; small ornamental gourd
Masking tape; tracing paper; scissors
Photocopier; soft and hard lead pencils
Colored pencils in dark burnt red and navy
Fine liner paintbrush; acrylic paints in
*   black, white, and gold*
Paper; small round paintbrush
Metallic acrylic paints in teal, purple,
*   dark green, lime green, gold tone, red,*
*   and blue; medium flat paintbrush*
Black velvet braid trim; white glue
Gold tone decorative lace; fabric stiffener
Hot-glue gun and sticks; rhinestones
Decorative fabric; needle and thread; rice
Plastic hands; small plastic boots
*   (available in the doll section of hobby*
*   and crafts stores); two-by-fours for base*
Nails; hammer; 1-inch insulating
*   plastic foam (available at home*
*   improvement centers)*
Fine gravel (available with the miniature
*   railroad supplies at hobby stores)*
Small rocks; strong adhesive, such as
*   Liquid Nails; glitter; sand*

king humpty

HERE'S HOW

1 Clean the gourd as described on *page 99* and shown in Photo A, *right*. To plan the face, draw lines to indicate the waist and hat lines. Estimate where arms, legs, and ears will go. Draw a temporary pencil line down the center of the face that will become the center of his nose. This will help in placing arms, legs, and ears. On this shape, his hat comes about one-fourth of the way down the gourd and his waist is about one-third of the way up from the bottom. The arms are immediately above the waist on the far left and right sides. The legs are positioned as far apart in front as possible without moving to the sides.

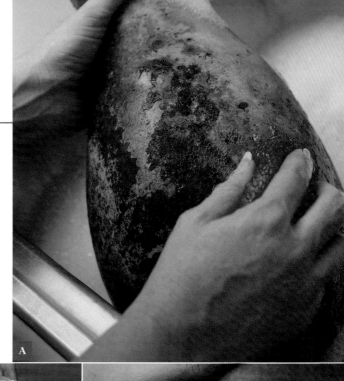

A

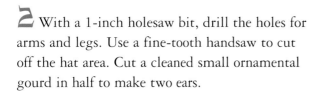

B

C

2 With a 1-inch holesaw bit, drill the holes for arms and legs. Use a fine-tooth handsaw to cut off the hat area. Cut a cleaned small ornamental gourd in half to make two ears.

3 Remove the dried insides. Discard or save the seeds if desired.

4 Stain the gourd as if staining a piece of wood. Brush on a wood stain such as oak or another dark, warm brown color. Let the stain soak in well and then wipe off with a rag. Let dry. Do the same for the small ornamental gourd.

5 Use wood glue to glue on the ears and the hat back on. Secure lightly with masking tape while the glue sets.

6 Trace the pattern, *page 102,* as a guide to draw the face. The size may need to be adjusted to accommodate the gourd. Make several photocopies in various sizes, cut out, and tape onto face until the size fits. Color the back side of pattern heavily with a soft lead pencil; tape the pattern, right side up, onto the face of the gourd. Draw over the pattern outline with a sharp, hard pencil, transferring the pattern onto the face of the gourd as shown in Photo B. Remove pattern.

7 Refer to the close-up face picture, *page 99,* as a guide for shading. Start with a dark burnt red colored pencil. Color in all shaded areas as

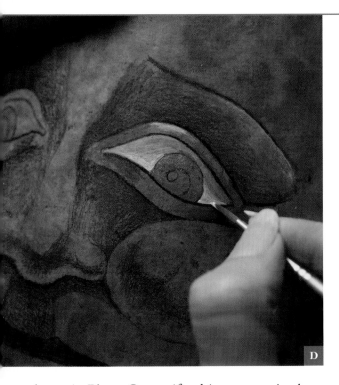

D

shown in Photo C even if red is not seen in the picture. Keep your pencils sharp. You will layer colors on top of each other. Work from dark to light, shading darker red from eyelid crease upward and outward to lighter red. Shade lower eyelids, lightening in the center. Shade in nose and cheeks to create a roundness. Shade under nose, heavily on the upper lip, and under the lower lip, on sides of the mouth, and on the bottom of the chin. Next add another layer of color using the dark navy pencil. Shade heavier in the darker corners, lightening your pencil coloring as you work outward. Color the darkest in the pattern line areas.

8 Thin a little black paint with water and fill fine liner brush with just enough paint to make a fine, smooth line, not dripping, thick, or heavy. Test your brush line first on paper. Accentuate all the facial lines by painting in black outlines, such as around eyelids, nose, cheeks, and mouth.

9 To paint the eyeballs, use metallic teal and metallic light green. Paint left sides of eyeballs

in teal and right sides in green. Thin the teal paint with water to make it transparent, one part water to one part paint. Paint a teal shadow with very little paint just under the upper eyelid line (in the whites of the eyes). Add a transparent teal shadow just under his nose and a little bit at the darkest corners of his cheeks (under eyes).

10 Paint in black pupils, outline eyeballs, and add to any dark lines that need more contrast.

11 With a little thinned white acrylic paint on your brush, paint the eyes as shown in Photo D. Add white highlights as shown on *page 99*. Use a small round brush to paint the most in lightest areas, fading the paint away into the dark areas. For example, on the eyebrows, paint the most white right next to the eyebrow and fade away as you paint downward into the shadow. Use paint very sparingly; additional layers can be added if the color is too weak. On the eyelids, paint the whitest highlights in the center, fading as you paint outward. On the whites of the eyes, paint the whitest toward the bottom, fading as you paint upward. Paint highlights on the bridge of the nose and the balls of the cheeks. Paint a faint highlight next to the dark line at the bottom of the nose and next to the dark line at the bottom of the cheeks. Highlight the bottom lip and the top of the chin. Paint two strong white highlights on the eyeballs by dipping the handle of the small paintbrush in undiluted white paint and dotting it onto the surface. Place the dots in the same position on each eyeball: upper left, right inside the black circle.

instructions continued on page 102

king humpty

12 If desired, add extra highlighting to give Humpty a more royal face. Use white acrylic paint with gold to add highlights around face. Thin paint with water and apply very sparingly. Highlight in light areas of eyebrows, nose, cheeks, bottom lip, and above eyebrows. Paint a white collar above waist.

13 To paint the clothing, paint the hat area solid metallic purple. Divide his seat area into sections and paint them metallic purple, blue, red, and dark green. Add dots, lines, and center motifs using a fine liner brush. Add detail by outlining in black. Paint dark green stripes on hat. Add lime green highlights and additional red stripes. Let paint dry.

14 Trim waist by gluing a piece of black velvet braid onto gourd. Glue another piece on bottom edge of head. Cut a piece of ornate gold lace to go around hat. Soak it with fabric stiffener. As it begins to dry, hot-glue it to the edge of hat. Glue rhinestones onto lace with white glue.

15 Trace two each of the arm and leg patterns, *opposite,* onto fabric. Cut out pieces, sew seams leaving the tops open, and turn right side out. Fill with rice and sew the top of each arm and leg shut.

16 Hot-glue the leg ends into the insides of the boots and the hands on the arms. Insert arms and legs into the holes and hot-glue in place.

KING HUMPTY FACE PATTERN

17 For the base, build a frame the desired size using two-by-fours. Cut foam sheets to fit all four sides. Nail in place. Cut a piece of foam slightly larger than top. Nail in place.

18 Coat top piece with white glue. Sprinkle fine gravel over glue. Let dry.

19 Paint rocks with diluted metallic paint. Let dry. Glue in place using adhesive. Paint white glue between rocks, working on one side at a time. Sprinkle with sand and glitter as shown in Photo E. Let dry. Repeat for each side.

**KING HUMPTY
FLOWER PATTERN**

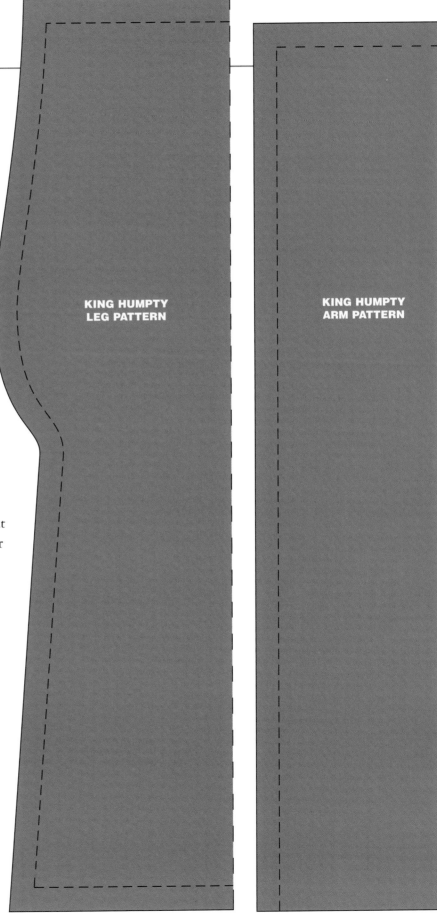

**KING HUMPTY
LEG PATTERN**

**KING HUMPTY
ARM PATTERN**

package pretties

THESE PACKAGE TRIMS ARE GIFTS IN
THEMSELVES. MADE FROM PAPIER-MÂCHÉ,
THE ORNAMENTS CAN BE TRANSFORMED INTO A WIDE
ASSORTMENT OF SHAPES SUITABLE FOR ANY OCCASION.

Papier-mâché is a fun medium to work with and a good learning tool for children.

For this project, you can enlarge the patterns *below*, draw your own, or use large cookie cutters. Keep in mind that the shapes are meant to look free-form, so allow the papier-mâché to maintain its texture.

Some papier-mâché mixtures are wetter than others. To protect your work surface from moisture, you may wish to work on waxed paper or a cookie sheet with sides.

Papier-mâché mix, such as Celluclay
Water; bowl
Tracing paper
Pencil
Waxed paper; ruler
Toothpick
Cord and string of beads
Metallic acrylic paints in deep blue, purple,
  and magenta
Acrylic paints in lime green, yellow, and orange
Medium flat paintbrush
Gold Rub 'n' Buff
Decorative ribbon

If you wish to hang your trims as ornaments, carefully make a hole with a toothpick or an awl before each piece dries. If a hole is desired after a piece dries, carefully drill a small hole with a hand drill.

instructions continued on page 106

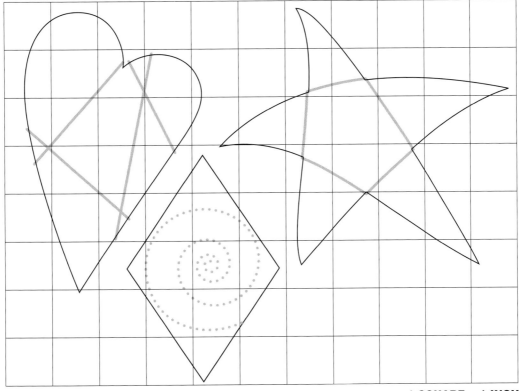

ORNAMENT PATTERNS   **1 SQUARE = 1 INCH**

package pretties

A

HERE'S HOW

1 Mix papier-mâché with enough water to form a workable dough, not too wet or thin.

2 Enlarge and trace the patterns, *page 105,* onto tracing paper. Lay waxed paper over tracing. Press papier-mâché onto shape as shown in Photo A. Form it into ornaments about ¼ inch thick. Use a toothpick to make a hole for hanging. Let sit until just dry enough to pick up and handle but not totally dry.

3 When you can handle the ornament, wrap cord or string of beads for texture around the ornament in a random pattern. Press firmly into ornament. Let dry completely.

4 Paint ornaments in different color schemes as shown in Photo B. You can apply layers of paint in the following colors: For heart, use deep blue, purple, magenta, and orange as shown in Photos C and D.

B

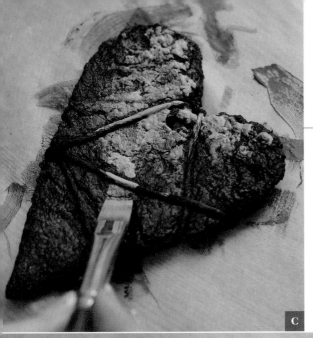

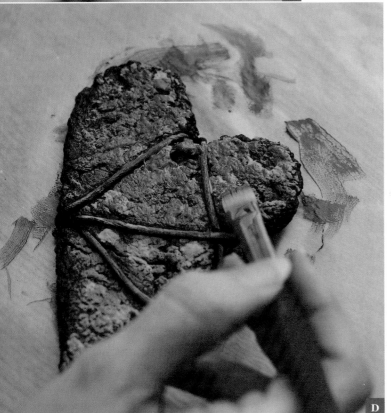

For the diamond, use purple, lime green, and yellow. For the star, use deep blue, purple, magenta, orange, and yellow. Paint the first layer thoroughly, filling crevices. Let it dry. Paint the second layer using less paint, allowing the crevices to remain the first color. With each layer of paint, use less paint and just highlight. Let dry.

5 With very little Rub 'n' Buff on finger, highlight across the raised areas and the cord as shown in Photo E. Gently rub gold color onto ornament.

6 Use decorative ribbon to tie trim to a package or to create a hanger for use as an ornament.

THESE PAPIER-MÂCHÉ SHAPES WOULD
BE BEAUTIFUL MOUNTED AND FRAMED.
JUST ELIMINATE THE HOLE FOR HANGING.

PAINTING PROJECTS
for the home

YOUR HOME IS YOUR CASTLE, AND, AS
AN ARTIST, YOU WANT YOURS TO REFLECT YOUR
IMAGINATIVE FLAIR AND INGENUITY.
THIS CHAPTER IS FILLED WITH IDEAS FOR
ADDING HAND-PAINTED TOUCHES TO EVERY ROOM WITH
UPLIFTING PROJECTS THAT WILL HELP YOU
ACHIEVE JUST THE LOOK YOU WANT, NO MATTER WHAT
YOUR DECORATING STYLE.

TIPS FOR PAINTING PROJECTS
for the home

GENERAL TIPS

More home accessories are available than ever before, which is heavenly for those who like to enhance their surroundings with personal artistic flair. Not only are there more decorating choices in general, but when you add in hand painting, the options are limitless.

In this chapter you'll discover fun new ways to spruce up walls, windows, and furniture in styles ranging from traditional to whimsical to contemporary.

PAINTING FURNITURE

When choosing furniture to paint, first check its stability and make any necessary repairs before painting. You may want to check the construction of a piece since it is easier to paint something disassembled. If you choose to do this, keep screws, hinges, and other hardware in a small plastic bag or container and make a list of where the pieces go. If necessary, make notes as you disassemble a piece so it can be put back together easily.

PAINTING WALLS

Consider where you are painting when selecting wall paint, even when doing only trim or detail work. If you're painting in a high-traffic area or you have small children, you may wish to use a washable paint.

Many brands of wall paint are available; just make sure you choose one that will meet your needs and give you the color, texture, and sheen desired. Most interior wall paints come in flat (least sheen), satin (slight sheen), and gloss (high sheen). Gloss paints are often the most durable, while flat paints show marks on the wall.

PAINTING ON FABRIC

When painting pillows, curtains, lampshades, or other fabric items, consider whether the item will ever have to be washed. If it does, be sure to use a washable fabric paint or acrylic paint mixed with textile medium.

To prevent paint from soaking through to other layers of fabric while painting, place waxed paper beneath the fabric layer being painted.

Follow the paint manufacturer's instructions, as some fabric paint needs to be heated by an iron to make it permanent.

HOW COLOR INFLUENCES MOOD

Wondering what color to paint your walls? Here are a few examples of how color influences mood:

- Pink: soothes, acquiesces; promotes affability and affection
- Yellow: expands, cheers; increases energy
- White: purifies, energizes, unifies; enlivens all other colors
- Black: disciplines, authorizes, strengthens; encourages independence
- Orange: cheers, commands; stimulates appetites, conversation, and charity
- Red: empowers, stimulates, dramatizes, competes; symbolizes passion
- Green: balances, normalizes, refreshes; encourages emotional growth
- Purple: comforts, spiritualizes; creates mystery and draws out intuition
- Blue: relaxes, refreshes, cools; produces tranquil feelings and peaceful moods

SELECTING PAINTBRUSHES

With all paintbrushes and rollers, you get what you pay for. If you're going to use a brush or roller only for a small project, a less expensive brush may do the job and can then be thrown away. But if you want your paintbrushes to last, consider buying good-quality brushes and take care when cleaning and storing them.

Foam paintbrushes come in handy when applying a variety of wall-painting techniques; however, the foam can catch on highly textured walls, leaving tiny pieces of foam on the wall. On the positive side, they're inexpensive and do not show brushstrokes.

funky folk-art tables

EVERYONE CAN USE AN EXTRA TABLE HERE AND

THERE, SO THESE BRIGHT RENDITIONS WON'T FIND

THEMSELVES IN THE CORNER FOR LONG.

1 These are simple little wooden tables with detachable legs. This design can be adapted to a square or rectangular table. First, remove legs. In a well-ventilated work area, prime tabletops with white spray primer. Let dry.

2 Enlarge and trace the bird table and additional patterns, *pages 114–115,* onto tracing paper. Cut out the wavy line pattern. Tape it to the table's edges, keeping the curves centered.

3 Paint in hot pink section, orange border, and lime green edges. Paint two coats if necessary. Let dry.

4 Transfer the birds onto pink area. Paint in yellow, lime green, orange, and lavender areas. Let dry.

5 Paint in small random hearts using medium black paint pen. Let dry. Paint inside the hearts with lavender, lime green, and yellow paint. Add dots and dashes as shown on pattern. To paint dots, dip the handle of paintbrush into paint and dot onto surface.

6 Use the paint pen to outline the birds and to make stripes.

7 To paint the heart table, paint the top yellow and the sides pink. Transfer heart pattern and finish painting as on bird table.

8 Paint wood hearts according to the patterns, *page 115,* and let dry. Glue the hearts together with wood glue. String black seed beads onto a length of beading wire or beading thread, leaving at least 3 inches on each end. Glue one end to the back of the heart and the other under the table. Reattach the legs to the table.

WHAT YOU'LL NEED

Wood tables
White spray primer, such as Kilz
Tracing paper
Pencil
Scissors
Tape
Acrylic paints in hot pink, orange, lime green, yellow, and lavender
Medium flat paintbrush; medium round paintbrush
Medium-point black paint pens
Small and medium wood hearts
Wood glue
Beading wire or thread
Black seed beads

HEART TABLE PATTERN

1 SQUARE = 1 INCH

**POLKA-DOT HEART
PATTERN**

**STRIPED HEART
PATTERN**

leaf-laden pillows

THESE NEUTRAL PILLOWS ARE SIMPLE IN PATTERN AND

IN TECHNIQUE. MAKE THE PRETTY PAIR YOURSELF

AND EMBELLISH A PAIR OF CURTAINS TO MATCH.

WHAT YOU'LL NEED

Scissors; measuring tape
Desired fabric for pillows
Iron
Tracing paper; soft lead pencil
Tape; disposable plate
Iridescent pearl white acrylic paint
Textile painting medium; flat paintbrush
Ivory fabric dimensional paint
Printer paper; crafts knife
Straight pins
Binding
Sewing machine; thread
Stuffing
Hand-sewing needle

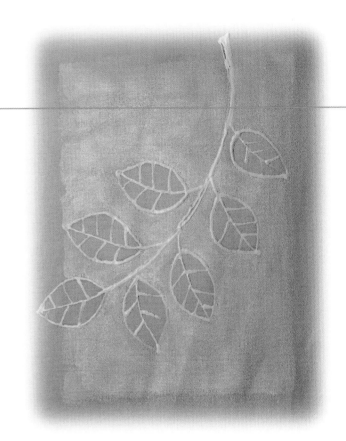

HERE'S HOW

1 Cut fabric pieces to desired size for pillows. Press and lay flat on work surface.

2 For the green pillow, trace leaf branch pattern, *page 118,* onto tracing paper. Color the back side with a soft lead pencil. Tape pattern down onto center of fabric. Draw around outline with a sharp pencil, transferring pattern onto fabric. Remove paper.

3 Place a small dab of acrylic paint on plate. Add one part textile medium to two parts paint. Mix together and brush onto fabric, avoiding inside of leaves. Let dry. Paint another coat if necessary. Let dry. Use fabric dimensional paint to outline leaves. Let dry.

4 For the ivory pillow, trace the falling leaves pattern, *page 119,* onto printer paper. Carefully cut out leaf shapes with a crafts knife.

5 Lay the stencil on fabric where desired. Paint inside leaves with acrylic paint, brushing from outside inward. Remove paper and repeat process until the entire fabric area is painted. You may paint over each leaf with a second coat without using the stencil. Let dry. Outline leaf shapes with fabric paint. Let dry.

6 Pin front side of pillow to back side with right sides facing, attaching decorative binding between two fabric pieces. Sew around all edges, leaving several inches open for stuffing; turn. Stuff pillow and sew opening closed with needle and thread.

leaf-loden pillows

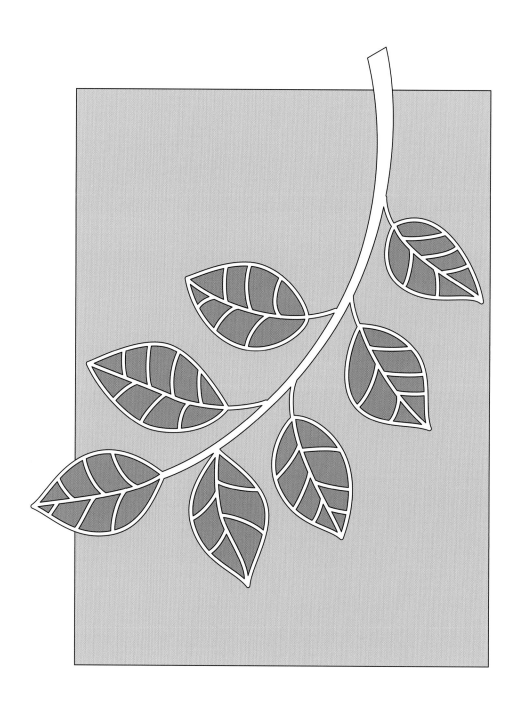

**LEAF ON BRANCH
PILLOW PATTERN**

118

**FALLING LEAVES
PILLOW PATTERN**

bright shade

TIPS BEFORE YOU BEGIN

WHAT YOU'LL NEED

When selecting a lampshade to paint, choose one made of fabric or heavy paper because acrylic paint may not adhere to some plastics. Also keep the shape in mind. In order for this roller technique to work, the surface has to be relatively flat.

instructions continued on page 122

Crafts knife
3-inch foam roller
Acrylic paints in raw sienna, yellow, and purple
Paint tray
Teaspoon; water
Spatula
Lampshade
Paper towels
Trim for top and bottom of shade
White glue

ENHANCE A LAMPSHADE WITH A PAINTING

TECHNIQUE THAT ADDS TEXTURE IN NATURAL TONES.

THIS LAMP SPORTS A SPLATTERING OF AUTUMN

COLORS, BUT YOU COULD CHANGE THE COMBINATION TO

REFLECT YOUR FAVORITE COLOR TRIO.

bright shade

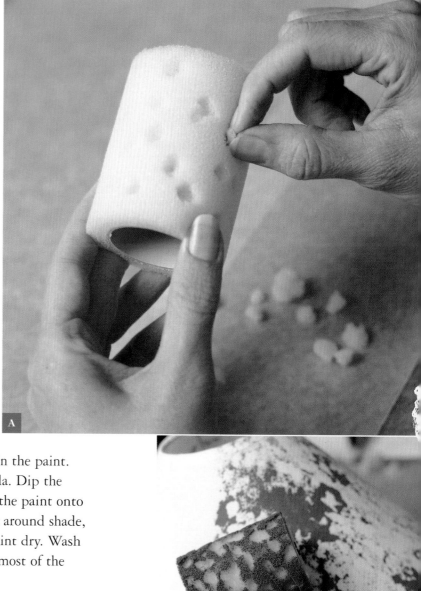

A

B

HERE'S HOW

1 Use a crafts knife to score short slashes all around the foam surface of the roller.

2 With fingers, pull out little pieces of foam next to each slash mark to create an irregular surface as shown in Photo A.

3 Begin with raw sienna and pour paint into paint tray. Add ¼ to ½ teaspoon water to slightly thin the paint. Mix the paint and water with a spatula. Dip the roller into the thinned paint and roll the paint onto the shade as shown in Photo B. Work around shade, applying strokes randomly. Let the paint dry. Wash the color from the roller and roll out most of the moisture on a pad of paper towels.

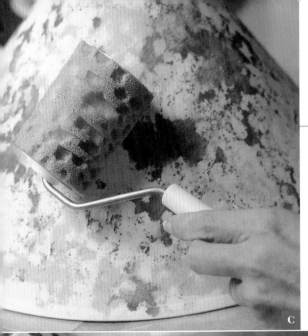

4 Apply yellow paint in the same manner and roll randomly over the shade as shown in Photo C. Let the paint dry. Clean the roller and dry it on a pad of paper towels.

5 Apply the final layer with purple paint. Use the edge of the roller to make purple streaks randomly around the shade as shown in Photo D. Let the paint dry.

6 Glue trim around the top and bottom edges of the shade. Let the glue dry.

WHILE WE'VE USED THIS TECHNIQUE ON A LAMPSHADE, YOU CAN ALSO USE IT TO LIVEN UP FURNITURE, WALLS, CURTAINS, OR NEARLY ANY FLAT SURFACE.

vineyard walls

TIPS BEFORE YOU BEGIN

Use silk leaves and plastic grapes to create a dimensional, sculptured look. Use your imagination and you'll find many other items that work well with this technique, such as lightweight shells, silk flowers, and other artificial fruits sliced in half.

instructions continued on page 126

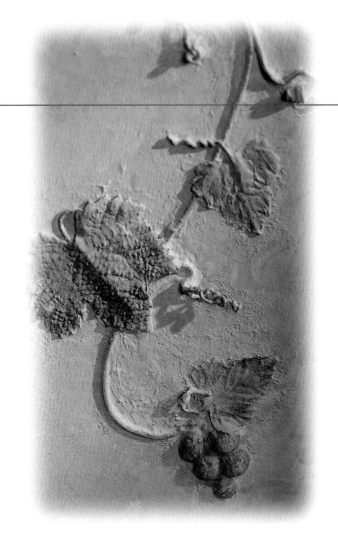

WHAT YOU'LL NEED

Artificial plastic grapes and leaves; scissors
Wire or smooth cord; 1-inch-wide paintbrush
*Texturing medium (available in fine-art
    paint section of crafts supply stores); wet cloth*
*Twin- or double-roller painting kit (available in
    paint and home improvement stores)*
Tan and ivory latex interior satin or flat paint
*Stencil creams in mauve, dark green, lavender,
    and yellow; stencil brush (available in paint,
    art and crafts supply stores)*

ADD ELEGANCE AND TEXTURE TO YOUR
WALLS USING THIS ELEGANT PAINT-ON-PLASTIC
TECHNIQUE. CUT ARTIFICIAL GRAPES IN HALF SO
THEY APPEAR TO BE EMBEDDED IN THE WALL.

HERE'S HOW

1 Remove plastic grapes and leaves from stems. Cut grapes in half using scissors. For stems, use wire or any kind of smooth cord.

2 Using a paintbrush, thickly apply texturing medium to the wall. Apply generously in the area where grapes are desired. Begin arranging the grapes in a cluster starting at the top and working downward. Place the smaller ones toward the bottom. Fill in some of the crevices between the grapes and around the outer edges, making it appear like a sculpture coming out of the wall. Use a wet cloth to blot around the edges to blend the texture into the wall.

A

3 Use the same technique with the leaves, also applying medium to front of leaf as shown in Photo A. Paint on more texturizing medium to cover grapes. Add curls of wire and cord, cover well with medium, and blend edges with wet cloth. Let dry until hard. It may take a couple of hours to dry, depending on how thickly the medium is applied.

4 Use a double roller with textured roller pads. Pour tan paint in one half of the paint tray (kit should include a paint tray containing two wells for paint) and ivory in the other half.

5 Using a 1-inch-wide brush, brush the darker color over the entire sculptured area as shown in Photo B. Then begin rolling the paint onto the wall.

B

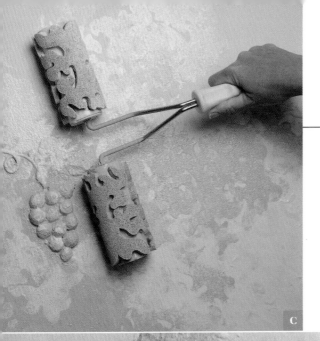

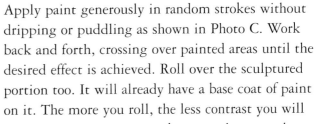

Apply paint generously in random strokes without dripping or puddling as shown in Photo C. Work back and forth, crossing over painted areas until the desired effect is achieved. Roll over the sculptured portion too. It will already have a base coat of paint on it. The more you roll, the less contrast you will see between the two colors. Use the small painting tools that come with the kit to work paint into the corners and edges. Let dry.

6 Use stencil cream to apply color tints to the leaves and grapes as shown in Photo D. Apply a tiny amount of dark green in the crevices of the grapes. Apply a little mauve on the left side of grapes, and apply lavender on the right. With a dry stencil brush, blend subtly together. Use very little cream. Gently buff off some color with a soft cloth if desired.

7 On the leaves, use green, mauve, and yellow in sparse amounts. Blend colors together, allowing some of each to remain unblended. The mauve will tone down the green. Let dry.

Note: If you wish to remove pieces from the wall, do so carefully with a putty knife. Patching of drywall may be needed.

textured surrounds

TIPS BEFORE YOU BEGIN

This technique enhances the wall texture and provides movement. So that your room does not get overly busy, consider placing the squares on one wall only, using the glazing technique on the remaining walls.

For already themed rooms, you may wish to adapt the design. Instead of squares, try fish, heart, star, or sunburst shapes. Just remember to turn the sponge so the shapes vary in their angles.

instructions continued on page 130

WHAT YOU'LL NEED

Deep golden ocher latex wall paint in flat, eggshell, or satin

Paintbrush

Glazes in deep red, plum, dark green, and lime green

3- or 4-inch-wide chip paintbrush (available in hardware and home improvement stores with the house painting brushes)

Water; damp cloth

Sponge for stamping

Scissors

Acrylic paints in dark green, gold ocher, and deep red

Disposable plate

RICH WITH COLOR AND TEXTURE,

THIS WALL TECHNIQUE DANCES WITH HANDSOME SQUARE

PATTERNS TWIRLING IN EVERY DIRECTION.

textured surrounds

A

HERE'S HOW

1 This technique works very well on a textured wall. First paint the wall a color similar to gold ocher. It may appear very bright at first, but the color will deepen and tone down with layers of glaze over it. Let dry.

2 Using a 3- or 4-inch chip brush, apply sections of glaze using dark green, lime green, deep red, and plum. Apply randomly as shown in Photo A.

3 Work in sections and work fairly quickly. Do not allow the glaze to dry before blending. Keeping chip brush clean, dip in water and blend the colors together. It is all right if the colors run a bit. There should be more glaze in some areas than others. Leave some areas just plum, red, or green but blend together over the ocher areas.

DON'T LET THE INTENSE COLORS STARTLE YOU.

THE GLAZES TONE DOWN AFTER THE PROCESS IS COMPLETE.

THEN YOU CAN STAMP ON AS MANY DESIGNS AS

DESIRED TO COMPLETE THE LIVELY LOOK.

4 Allow the glaze to sit and soak in somewhat but do not let dry. Use a damp cloth to wipe over glaze. Wipe more in some areas than others as shown in Photo B. The more you wipe, the more gold color will show through. When finishing a section at a time, do not leave a hard edge. Wipe gradually into the unglazed ocher area.

5 After glazed wall is dry, begin stamping. Cut a 1¾-inch square from sponge for the ocher. Cut a 1-inch square from the center to use for the dark green (leaves a frame-shape sponge for ocher). Cut a separate ½-inch square for the red. Apply in three layers, starting with the green. Spread green acrylic paint onto plate, dip the 1-inch square into green, and stamp onto wall as shown in Photo C. Practice a few times on paper if desired. Let dry. Next, use frame-shaped sponge, dip into gold ocher, and stamp over the green. Last, stamp the small square sponge in red and apply in the center of the green square. Let dry.

blooming valance

PLANT A ROW OF PANSIES ALONG THE SCALLOPED
EDGE OF A VALANCE. THE SPLATTERED BACKGROUND
IS CREATED BY SQUIRTING ON STRIPES OF PAINT
FROM A SPRAY BOTTLE. SEED BEADS AND CORD ADD THE
FINISHING TOUCHES.

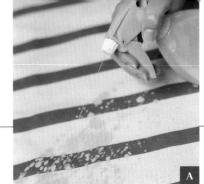

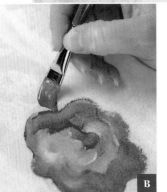

HERE'S HOW

Paper; pencil; scissors; unlined, straight valance in
    desired length; measuring tape
Lining fabric; straight pins
1-inch-wide blue masking tape; waxed paper
Acrylic paints in yellow-gold, bright pink, pink,
    leaf green, mint green, and black
Liquid textile medium (available with the
    acrylic paint in crafts and discount stores)
Spray bottle; disposable plate
Fine liner paintbrush
Large black seed beads; black thread; needle
Thread to match lining; white satin cord

1 Cut a paper scallop pattern approximately 8 inches wide. Trace the scallop along the bottom edge of the valance, leaving ¼ inch of fabric at the valance bottom.

2 Place a vertical strip of masking tape between each scallop. Leaving 3 inches in the center of each scallop, place a strip of masking tape on each side.

3 Cover work surface with waxed paper. Lay valance, right side up, on waxed paper. Mix yellow-gold paint with textile medium as directed by the textile medium manufacturer. Place about ½ cup into a clean spray bottle. Spray the entire valance randomly with paint mixture, allowing the white fabric to show through the paint splatters. If desired, avoid painting the hanging tabs. Let dry. Remove tape.

4 On a disposable plate, mix bright pink, pink, leaf green, and mint green paints with textile medium. To make a flower on each scallop, paint baseball-size circles 1½ inches from the edge using bright pink and pink. Paint bumpy edges to create petals.

5 To paint leaves, use leaf and mint green. Paint two leaves for each flower, placing in different areas if desired. Let dry.

6 Mix black paint with textile medium. Use a fine liner paintbrush to add line details to the flowers and leaves. Let dry. Sew three black seed beads in each flower center.

7 Cut a lining piece ½ inch larger than valance. Trim the valance ¼ inch beyond the scallop line. Trace this scallop along one long edge of the lining. Cut out. With right sides together, sew the scallop edges of the valance and lining together. Clip the seam and turn right side out. Fold the lining fabric edges to meet those of the valance. Pin in place. Hand-sew the edges together.

8 Using a needle and thread, hand-tack the cord to the scalloped edge as shown.

leaf-print table

BRING TRACES OF THE OUTDOORS IN WITH THESE
LEAF-IMPRESSIONED TABLES. MADE TO LOOK LIKE STONE,
THIS TABLETOP IS CRAFTED FROM CLAY.

Make this project one for the family by getting everyone involved right from the start. Go on a nature walk to collect items to press into the clay.

When selecting leaves, pinecones, acorns, and other items, look for intact shapes. Store the items flat (placing them in a phone book works well) until you are ready to use them.

Another way to give this table one-of-a-kind flair is by selecting an unusual table base. Check a flea market or garage sale for antique tables, wrought-iron bases, or bases from old sewing machines.

instructions continued on page 136

½ inch plywood cut to desired tabletop size
Rolling pin
White oven-bake clay, such as Sculpey; knife
*Assorted leaves, acorns, pinecones, and other
    nature items*
Pencil or marker
Baking dish
*Oil paints in red, magenta, yellow, brown,
    and green; disposable plate*
Stiff medium flat paintbrush
Cloth
Clear matte or satin varnish
Strong adhesive, such as E6000
Grout
Leather trim to go around edge
Crafts knife
Tiny nails; hammer
Table base

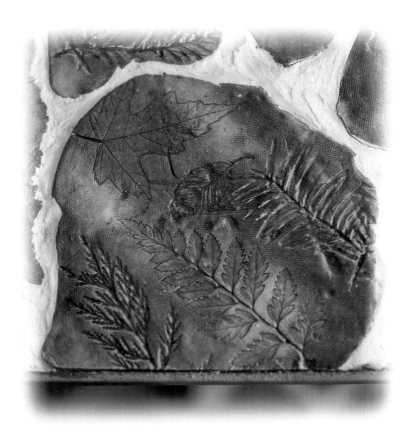

leaf-print table

HERE'S HOW

I Roll out irregularly shaped
pieces of white clay to about
⅛ inch thick. Arrange leaves and
items on clay. Roll the rolling pin
gently over items, pressing just
enough to make an impression as
shown in Photo A. Remove leaves
from clay and lay clay onto wood
tabletop. Let the clay hang over at
the table edge. Continue this
process and arrange pieces onto
table until it is full. Allow enough
room to grout in between pieces.
Trim overlapping clay along edges
of wood.

A

2 Draw an outline with pencil or
marker around each piece of clay
as shown in Photo B. This will help you reposition the
pieces after you bake them.

3 Refer to your clay manufacturer's instructions and bake in
baking dish in oven until done. Let each piece cool and
remove from dish.

4 Arrange oil paints on a plate. Dip a stiff medium flat
paintbrush in paint and dab small dots of color randomly
onto the baked clay pieces as shown in Photo C. Use very
little paint on the clay. Begin to blend the colors together with
the brush, working paint well into the crevices. Occasionally
clean the brush. The paint should be thin and rather dry in
appearance, and blend fairly well into the clay. It is OK to
see brushstrokes. Let the paint begin to dry. This may take
a few hours, a day, or days depending on the conditions.
When the paint begins to dry, buff with a cloth as shown
in Photo D. It should smooth out the color even more,
eliminating brushstrokes but leaving most of the color. Let
the clay pieces dry completely. This could take days or weeks.

B

C

D

5 Apply at least four coats of clear matte or satin varnish to each piece. Allow to dry between coats.

6 Using the outline drawings as a guide, use a strong adhesive to affix each piece to the wood. Use a generous amount of adhesive, covering the entire back side of each piece of clay.

7 Mix grout according to directions, and grout areas between clay pieces. Press firmly to fill all crevices. Some may overlap onto clay pieces. Use more caution than you would with typical grout projects. The clay pieces are not as durable as fired ceramic, so be gentle and avoid scrubbing the abrasive grout off surface. Let grout dry. Use a soft cloth and plenty of water to wipe off surfaces of clay pieces.

8 Trim the edge of plywood clay pieces and tile with a leather strip or other desired material. Use a crafts knife to angle each corner 45 degrees so the corners of the strip butt evenly. Attach the strip with adhesive and reinforce the corners with tiny nails if necessary. Attach the tabletop to a base of choice.

dragonfly curtains

TIPS BEFORE YOU BEGIN

Select solid curtains that are somewhat sheer and at least half cotton so the paint will absorb and not bleed.

When stamping more than one panel, lay them side by side so you can plan the placement of the dragonflies for the entire window. You may want the design to be random or symmetrical. Make this decision before beginning to stamp the curtains.

DRAGONFLY PATTERN   **1 SQUARE = 1 INCH**

WHAT YOU'LL NEED

Tracing paper
Pencil; scissors
Foam rubber insoles for shoes
White glue
7×7-inch piece of $\frac{1}{2}$-inch-thick wood
Screen door handle; 2 screws; screwdriver
Iron; lightweight tab curtains
Scrap paper; pins; 4 food cans
Acrylic paint in bluegrass, purple, and copper
Paint tray
Paint spatula
Damp cloth
Paintbrushes
Gold puff paint

instructions continued on page 140

CAREFREE DRAGONFLIES TAKE FLIGHT ON THIS PAIR OF
OFF-WHITE CURTAINS. THE MUTED COLORS MAKE IT APPEAR
AS IF THE WINGED FRIENDS ARE FLUTTERING JUST OUTSIDE
THE WINDOW. THIS QUICK-PRINT TECHNIQUE ADDS A DESIGNER
TOUCH TO OTHERWISE ORDINARY WINDOW COVERINGS.

dragonfly curtains

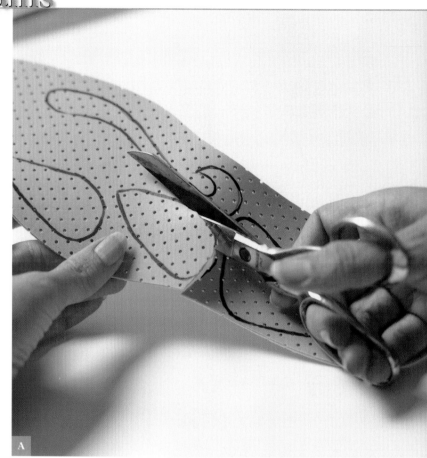

HERE'S HOW

1 Enlarge and trace the pattern, *page 139.* Cut out. Trace around the pattern pieces on the insoles. Cut out as shown in Photo A. With white side up, glue the pieces onto the block of wood as shown in Photo B. Let dry. Screw the door handle to the opposite side of block. Set aside.

2 Iron all creases out of curtain. Use the dragonfly pattern to cut out 10 dragonflies from scrap paper. Lay and pin dragonflies in position over curtain panel.

3 To prepare curtain for printing, lay the curtain, a section at a time, on a flat surface. Slip a piece of paper under the pinned dragonfly. Smooth the fabric flat and use four food cans (or other weight) to help hold the fabric flat around the area to be printed.

4 Randomly dribble purple and bluegrass paint in paint tray. Use paint spatula to smooth edges of the two paints together without mixing the paints too much.

5 Holding onto the handle, place wood block down into paint. Reposition block over paint in another direction. Check block to be sure all of the design is covered with an even, flat coat of paint as shown in Photo C. If necessary, use paint spatula to spread paint to all sections. Also wipe off any paint on the background wood with a damp cloth.

6 Use a paintbrush to apply splotches of copper paint to each wing on the pattern.

7 Position the wood block over the paper dragonfly, remove pin and paper dragonfly, and press wood block firmly onto fabric. Lift up the wood block as shown in Photo D. A paintbrush can be used to fill in any areas that did not print.

8 Continue this process, moving a new section of the curtain into position, smoothing and weighting the fabric. Each dragonfly will print differently, which is part of the charm of this method.

9 When all dragonflies have been printed, let the paint dry. Use gold puff paint to add two eyes to each dragonfly head.

AFTER YOUR CURTAINS ARE GRACING YOUR WINDOWS,
USE YOUR PRINTING BLOCK TO MAKE A
COORDINATING TABLECLOTH AND
NAPKINS FOR THE KITCHEN TABLE.

happy table & chair

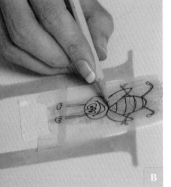

HERE'S HOW

1 Begin with a clean and dry table and chair. Sand any rough spots. Wipe off dust with a tack cloth.

2 Prime with white spray primer. Spray one or two coats, allowing to dry in between.

3 Paint entire surface a cream color. Paint two coats using a 2-inch-wide flat paintbrush. Allow to dry in between coats.

4 Plan where motifs are desired on the table. Trace patterns, *pages 145–147,* onto tracing paper. Color the back of character and flower patterns with soft pencil. Tape down patterns right side up. Use some or all of these patterns. Using a photocopier will make it much easier to copy the patterns, especially the words. Cut out letters with crafts knife to make a stencil. Save the inner portions of the A's and P's. Apply a tiny dab of rubber cement to backs of those portions. Tape down letter stencils where desired.

instructions continued on page 144

Table and chair
Sandpaper
Tack cloth
White spray primer, such as Kilz
Cream-colored acrylic paint
2-inch flat paintbrush
Tracing paper
Pencil; tape
Photocopier
Crafts knife; rubber cement
Small and medium round and flat brushes
Pastel-colored acrylic paints; disposable plate
Liner paintbrush
Needletip paint bottle for outlining
Glitter paint in bottle; scrap paper
Heavy gloss glaze sealer; casting resin
Disposable glass or tin container for mixing
Newspapers; crafts sticks

SKIP THE TIME-OUT CHAIR—THIS ONE IS DEFINITELY "IN"! WHOEVER SITS AT THIS ADORABLE SET WILL BE ENCOURAGED TO SMILE. COMPLETED IN SUBTLE PASTELS, THESE COMICAL DESIGNS ARE AS HAPPY AS CAN BE.

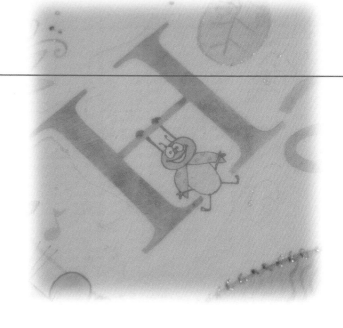

5 Arrange pastel colored paints on plate in small dabs. Paint letters first. Use very little paint in a stiff, small flat brush, or use a stencil brush. Brush a little paint off on scrap paper to make sure there isn't too much paint on the brush. The paint should go on almost dry. If there is too much paint on the brush, it will seep under the stencil. Brush from the outside inward. Paint each letter a different color. Let dry. Remove the stencils.

6 Transfer the other patterns onto the table. Trace around outline with a sharp, hard pencil. Remove paper. Paint in figures with pastel colors. Use small and medium round brushes and fine liner brush for details. Let dry.

7 Outline the desired figures with an outlining tool (a small plastic bottle with a needle tip made to hold paint). Mix paint a little thinner than the consistency of light cream. Test on scrap paper first. If it is too thin, it will run out. If it is too thick, it may not come out at all.

8 Paint the edges of table with small blocks of different colors.

9 Use glitter fabric paint to add sparkles around figures. Let dry.

10 Paint chair using the same techniques. Paint spindles different colors. Let dry.

11 Spray legs and spindles with a heavy-gloss glaze sealer.

12 The finish on the tabletop and chair seat is a casting resin. In a well-ventilated work area, mix the resin according to product directions. Place table on newspapers. Pour resin onto the surface of the table or chair, smoothing with a crafts stick. Smooth off any drips from the edges of table or chair seat. Let dry thoroughly. It may take several hours or days to dry depending on humidity. Add more coats to the tabletop and seat until the dimensional glitter paint no longer can be felt on the surface.

HAPPY CHAIR PATTERNS

HAPPY TABLE PATTERNS

1 SQUARE = 1 INCH

PAINTING
just for fun

LET YOUR IMAGINATION GO WILD WITH
SENSATIONAL PROJECTS THAT PROVIDE A PALETTE FULL
OF FUN. FROM PAINTING FIREPLACE LOGS
TO CREATING SPIN-ART PLACE MATS, YOU'LL HAVE
A GREAT TIME LEARNING NEW TECHNIQUES AND WAYS
TO SHOW OFF YOUR PAINTING SKILLS.

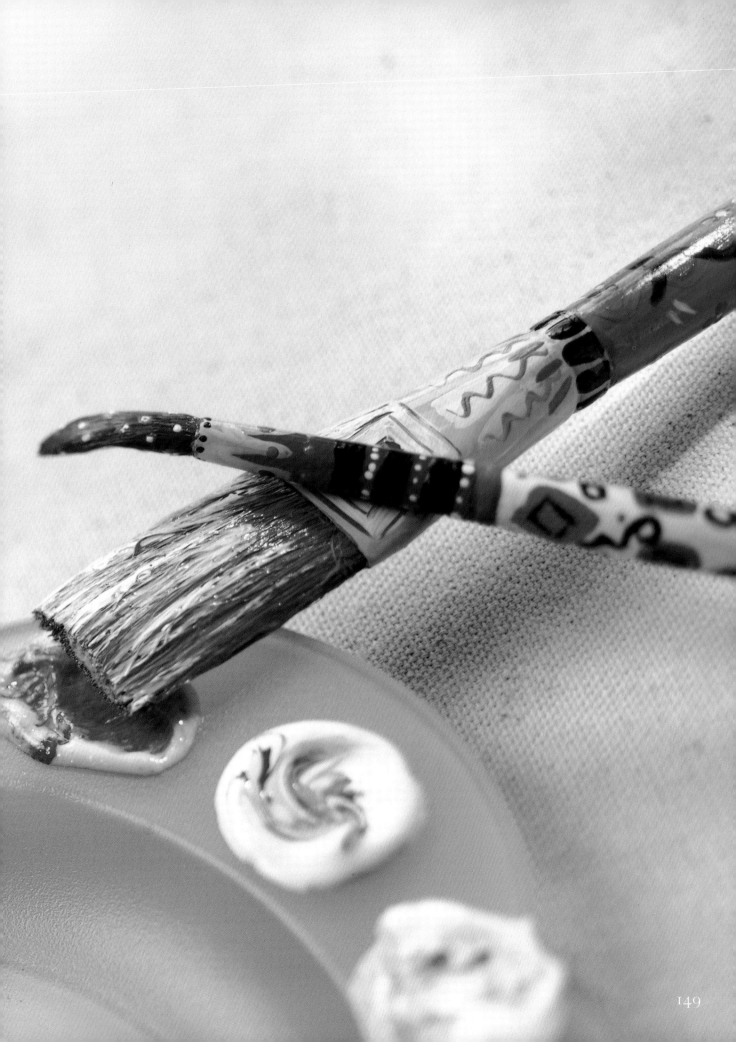

TIPS FOR PAINTING
just for fun

STRETCHING YOUR IMAGINATION

When you have the urge to grab your brushes and paint something new, try to go beyond the basics and what you have already mastered.

Page through this book to find a new technique you want to give a go, a product you've been itching to try, or a surface you have yet to conquer. It's so much fun to experiment with paint. And with all the available products out there, the possibilities are endless.

PLAY WITH COLOR

If you have a limited palette, you may want to consider adding some new hues. Most paints are relatively inexpensive, and color alone can open the door to new and exciting projects.

If you paint projects to give away or sell, consider making duplicates in a variety of color schemes. Try the same project in natural tones, primaries, and brights. Each color scheme will attract different types of people.

Drying can change the color of paint. Usually paint dries to a darker shade. For 99 percent accuracy, test-paint on nonabsorbent white paper and allow it to dry. Sheen changes color value as well. A flat matte paint differs in value from the same color in a shiny, glossy finish. The shinier the color, the lighter it will look.

Texture also alters color. Smooth surfaces reflect light, so a heavily textured wall will appear darker than a smooth wall painted the same color.

KEEP AN ARTFUL EYE

Watch for items that would come alive with paint. In this chapter you'll discover everything from logs to brooms, plastic masks to purchased linens—each turned into wonderful works of art by adding paint using various techniques. Once you're in this mind-set, you'll be amazed at how differently you shop or what you look for on nature hikes.

ADDING TEXTURE

You can always paint something to look textured, but consider adding a texture to a surface before painting. Here are some fun textures you can glue onto a surface before you put your paintbrush into action:

- Clay
- Pasta
- Sand
- Beads
- Sandpaper
- Dried leaves
- Dried flowers
- Gesso
- Torn paper pieces

The list could go on and on! Have fun experimenting before taking on a whole project.

USEFUL VS. VISUAL PLEASERS

Some items in this chapter, such as the brooms and place mats, have a use. Others are JUST FOR FUN! Keep the end use in mind when creating your painted pieces. This may help determine whether a piece needs to be sealed and will guide you in color selection.

Take the techniques shown in this book and try applying them to other projects. For instance, look at the clay-covered mask, *above left*. Wouldn't this technique look fantastic on a lamp base? Or consider the painted broom handles on *page 152*. Imagine these sweet designs on hand mirrors, table legs, or bedposts!

While all of your experiments may not turn out as planned, you may well happen across a new technique that feeds your painting passion like never before. After all, painting is about expressing your individual creativity and having FUN!

clean sweeps

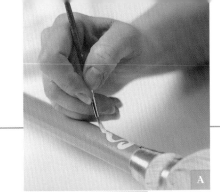

Broom with wood handle
Plastic bag
Masking tape
Spray paint in desired color
Acrylic paints in two shades of green and
  other desired colors
Small paintbrush
Pencil with round-tip eraser
Spray acrylic sealer

HERE'S HOW

1 To protect the broom straws from being painted, place a plastic bag over the end. Tape it tightly just below where the handle is attached.

2 In a well-ventilated work area, spray-paint the wood handle of the broom. Let it dry.

3 Using two different shades of green, paint wavy vines all the way around the broom handle as shown in Photo A. To make the vines, lay the straw portion of the broom in your lap and flip it constantly as you let the brush flow up the handle. Use one color first and let dry. Paint on the second vine color, letting the two shades of green overlap each other. Let the paint dry.

4 To make flowers, dip a pencil eraser in bright-colored paint and paint a circle of dots to create a flower as shown in Photo B. Put a contrasting dot in the center. Paint flowers scattered all over the handle as if they are growing on the vine. Let dry.

5 In a well-ventilated work area, spray the broom handle with acrylic sealer. Let dry.

A GREAT PROJECT TO MAKE AND GIVE AS

A HOUSEWARMING GIFT. OR PRESENT IT TO

THE PERSON WHO HAS EVERYTHING.

NOT MANY PEOPLE HAVE A DESIGNER,

HAND-PAINTED BROOM TO USE AT THEIR LEISURE.

153

so-hot logs

TOO PRETTY TO BURN, THESE FIREPLACE LOGS ADD
A PLAYFUL TOUCH TO ANY HEARTH. CHOOSE PAINT COLORS
TO MATCH YOUR DECOR; THEN ADD AS MUCH
(OR AS LITTLE) EMBELLISHMENT AS DESIRED.

HERE'S HOW

FOR THE STRIPED LOGS

1 Sand each log smooth. Remove dust with a tack cloth. In a well-ventilated work area, spray each log with primer. Let dry.

2 Using desired paint colors, paint simple, designs on the logs, such as stripes, zigzags, and dots. Vary the sizes of the elements so the piece is not overly busy. Leave two or three logs solid for contrast. Let dry.

3 Coat each log with varnish. Let dry. Where desired, wrap gold or silver wire around the logs as shown, *opposite.*

4 Stack the logs in a pleasing arrangement. Attach the logs using dowels. To do this, find an area on each log where it can be drilled on the back, and match it with a hole on the front of a touching log. Use short pieces of dowel to connect the logs. Use wood glue in each hole for extra support. Let dry.

5 For the flames, enlarge and trace the pattern, *above.* Cut out the shape. Trace around the shape on Plexiglas. Use screws to attach flames to the backs of the logs.

FOR THE SOLID LOGS

1 Place the logs in an interesting arrangement, with a large piece as the base and smaller pieces on top. Determine what color to paint each log. Keep in mind to place contrasting colors next to each other.

2 Mix each paint color with water, one part each. Test a small area on the wood. The paint should look like stain with the wood grain showing through. Paint each log and let dry.

3 Coat each log with varnish. Let dry. Stack the logs as planned. If desired, attach the logs using dowels as in Step 4, *above.*

4 For the flames, paint wood scraps and nail them to the back of the logs.

WHAT YOU'LL NEED

FOR BOTH SETS OF LOGS

Sandpaper; tack cloth; 6 fireplace logs for solid logs
6 aspen logs for striped logs; spray primer paint
3 or 4 bright water-based paints (such as acrylic,
*   watercolor, or tempera)*
Large flat paintbrush; water-based gloss wood varnish
Silver or gold wire; wire cutters; drill, dowels, wood
*   glue, and saw, optional; tracing paper; scissors*
Plexiglas and screws or wood scraps, optional

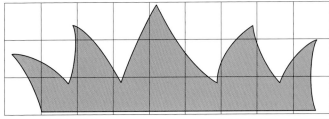

FLAME PATTERN **1 SQUARE = 1 INCH**

155

mother nature mask

CASTING AN ILLUSION OF LEATHER, THE MODELING ON
THIS MASK IS CREATED BY DRAWING DESIGNS IN TEXTURE
MEDIUM BEFORE APPLYING PAINT AND ANTIQUING GEL.

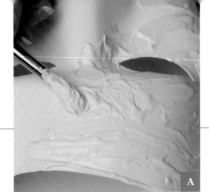

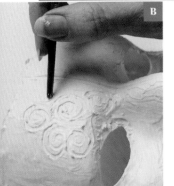

Plastic mask form with open top
Pencil; cardboard; scissors
Hot-glue gun and glue sticks
Texture medium (available in the fine-art paint
*   section of art and crafts supply stores)*
Paintbrush; toothpick
Acrylic paint in light terra-cotta
Brown antique gel; rag; raffia
Feathers; silk leaves; wheat; flowers
Jute or rope; hanger for back

HERE'S HOW

1 Trace outline of mask shape onto cardboard. Cut out cardboard ¼ inch beyond the pencil line.

2 Hot-glue mask onto cardboard, leaving ¼ inch extra cardboard around edge. The top will remain open.

3 Spread an even coat of texture medium onto mask with brush as shown in Photo A. Use a toothpick to scratch pattern or texture into medium as shown in Photo B. Draw the heavier lines with paintbrush handle. Let dry.

4 Paint mask light terra-cotta as shown in Photo C. Let the paint dry.

5 Brush on antique gel over the entire surface. When set but not completely dry, wipe off the excess with rag, leaving brown color in recessed areas as shown in Photo D.

6 Insert a generous amount of raffia into the open space at the top of mask, allowing it to overflow around face. Add stem of wheat, flowers, leaves, and feathers.

7 Hot-glue jute or rope trim onto the remaining cardboard edge. Attach a hanger to the back.

spinart place mats

MEALTIME WILL BE SO MUCH MORE FUN
WITH THESE FESTIVE SPIN-ART LINENS BECKONING
ALL TO THE TABLE. PAPER PLACE CARDS
ADD A GRAND FINALE.

I Prepare the work surface by covering it with waxed paper. Press the place mats and napkins if necessary. Decide where the paint prints will be placed.

2 Choose colors that will work well with the color of place mats and napkins chosen. Following the manufacturer's directions, place a piece of card stock into the paint toy. Add each color of paint and let it swirl. When you like the design, quickly remove it from the spinning mechanism and invert it onto the place mat to print the design. Repeat the process again to make multiple prints on the place mat if desired. Repeat for the napkin. Let dry. Keep card stock prints; after they dry, write names on them to use as place cards.

Waxed paper
Purchased place mats and napkins in desired colors; iron
Purchased paint swirl art toy (available at toy stores); card stock
Acrylic or fabric paints in desired colors
Fine line black permanent marker

index

project designers

Susan Banker 10, 14, 20, 28, 40, 56,
   78, 132
Carol Dahlstrom 84, 158
Phyllis Dunstan 34, 120, 138
Alexa Lett 152
Alice Wetzel 24, 30, 44, 48, 52, 62,
   70, 76, 80, 92, 96, 98, 104, 112,
   116, 124, 128, 134, 142, 156
Mary Williams 154

photo styling

Carol Dahlstrom

photo styling assistant

Donna Chesnut